In memory of my Mum and Dad who created me.

SO WHERE DO WE START??? WHERE SHOULD I START???......OH YEAH WE START AT THE BEGINNING..........

My name is Karen Jane. My Mum always told me that I was supposed to be christened Jane Karen. What's in a name? Who actually loves the name they were given. Who would rather be called something else, something exciting such as Mercedes, Fern or Hope. A name that is different to everyone else's. Today there are names that are trending that you should name your child. As sheep we follow when we cannot be inventive ourselves. Like Peach or Prince. Ha Ha well, it's the 1960s and it appears that there were a lot of babies born and christened Karen. I was one of them, I am okay with that I have been called worse. My ex husband had nick names for me over the 28 years we were married. Lilo Lil and Maud which I hated as it made me feel old, ancient and past my best. He did call me Love but very rarely did he call me by my name Karen. I was called Kal by my mum and of course we all get our full names when we are in trouble. I have been called Kaz, Kags, Honey, Lovely and more. I am Karen. At one point I used to spell my name Karren, to make it a bit more exciting and different. I carried on with Karren until I finally grew up. My middle name Jane. Well why couldn't it have been spelt Jayne, that would have been different. No, I was boring Karen Jane Edge. The title of my book Karen Jane came from....Nee Edge, married Dohren. I don't belong to those names anymore. The latter is painful, the first has also been painful. Hence the title Karen Jane. I decided to write this book firstly for my children, so they can understand the person I became. Secondly to rid myself of demons of my mixed up life. Thirdly to help others who may have gone through similar experiences. Lastly its helped me to come to terms with the weird, strange, sad, happy, ups and downs of my life.

I owe it to myself to accept what I have been through and what I will go through before I die.

It is a legacy for my children.

I hope you will understand, comprehend and relate to this story of my life. It is a story that will only take you and me so far. It has taken me years of my life to complete for various reasons. Purely because at times I couldn't put myself through the painful recalls and at times I have been on a tangent. I live in hope that you will enjoy this book, relate to it and most of all I want my children and others to understand the reasons that I am the person I was born and the person I became through the life experiences I have encountered from birth to the day I finished this book. It took me great effort, a lot of thought and research. A lot of revalidation of my life so far. Sometimes distressing, but above all fruitful and stronger. Everyone has a book inside of them, it just takes courage to write it and of course a long time. It maybe good it maybe crap. Please enjoy.

I would like to introduce you to two extremely important people in my life. If it wasn't for them I wouldn't be here, I would have not been able to write this book.

First up is my Dad. I have no pictures of my Dad as a baby as a child or of him growing up into a young man. I guess it was different then, people didn't take photos as we do today. Today people take pictures of almost everything, food, nights out, holidays and moments in their life. I feel I am very lucky to have photograph albums of my children growing up which I hold very dear. Today they are held on our phones, in danger of being lost forever. My Dad was called Frank. Just one name no middle name. Simple. He was of average build, average height. He had huge hands. We would joke by calling him banana fingers. He had black, thick, wavy hair which was controlled by brill cream. He had brown twinkling eyes that shone when he smiled. He was always clean shaven, dressed smartly. He was extremely handsome in a film star kind of way. He had lots of friends and was a likable man. My Dad frequented the local pubs drinking with like minded men of that era. He often came home too late for tea, missing tea completely. When he did arrive home he smelt of beer or gin. After drinking for most of his time he had a way of rubbing my mum up the wrong way when he did eventually arrive home. I am sure they were in love at one point. Frank never seemed to come across as being responsible for his role as a dad or a husband. He seemed to be unable to take on his father role. As if he never wanted to be tied down with a wife and children. Generally, he came and went when he pleased. This is only based on my memories others may think and say differently. My dad had a violent streak in him. If my mum was mad at him for coming home late or not providing house keeping, there would be war. He wasn't at home very much when he was he didn't contribute much generally. He was regularly making home brew using empty Barr soda bottles often drinking the home brew before it had time to ferment. Dad often came home with random things he had bought from sellers from the pub. G strings for my mum...... A David Soul album for my birthday, I didn't even like David Soul. A dog who we didn't have for very long before it mysteriously disappeared. Personally for me I think he should never got married or had children. He was a very private man. It wasn't until my 50s that I learnt so much more about the man I called DAD. Sadly. He died in 2014 from Dementia.

My mum. I have no pictures of my mum as a baby or as a child. This is how I remember my mum. She had so much hair, it was beautiful, shiny and quite striking. She would often scoop it up into a swinging pony tail. The pony tail would swing with every movement she made. Her eyes were a deep dark brown, wide glowing with life, with crinkles at the sides when she smiled, showing her pearly white teeth. Mum had an infectious laugh, like a naughty school girl laugh. She wasn't tall she wasn't small she was just right. She was slender with all the right curves in all the places they should be. I could see why my dad fell for her on their first meeting. My mum was strong, independent, caring and kind. She also had a nasty streak if you happened to get on the wrong side of her. I would witness this when I was older as she wrapped my brothers on their knuckles with a fork or with her hand that had her wedding ring on. I didn't witness any smacking or hitting with hands of my older brothers and I was never touched. Mum was funny, bright, cheery and very chatty. She always seemed to be working, she always had a little local job.

She loved gardening, she would often be seen weeding her borders. She was a massive Bingo Queen. My mum kept us well provided for, well dressed even though a lot of our clothes came from charity shops or jumble sales. We were always given presents at Christmas, annual holidays, food on the table. Our house was warm and we slept in our own cosy bed.

We didn't receive cuddles or kisses. We were never told that we were loved by either of our parents.

It was only when I was in my fifties when my parents told me that they loved me and gave me the odd hug.

It was only when I became a parent myself that I realised that parenting doesn't always come naturally. We do what we think is right for our children and I believe we also learn from our parent's mistakes.

Maybe it wasn't the done thing then, nevertheless I loved my parents. Sadly. My Mum died unexpectedly in 2021. I still miss her terribly and miss everything about this wonderful woman.

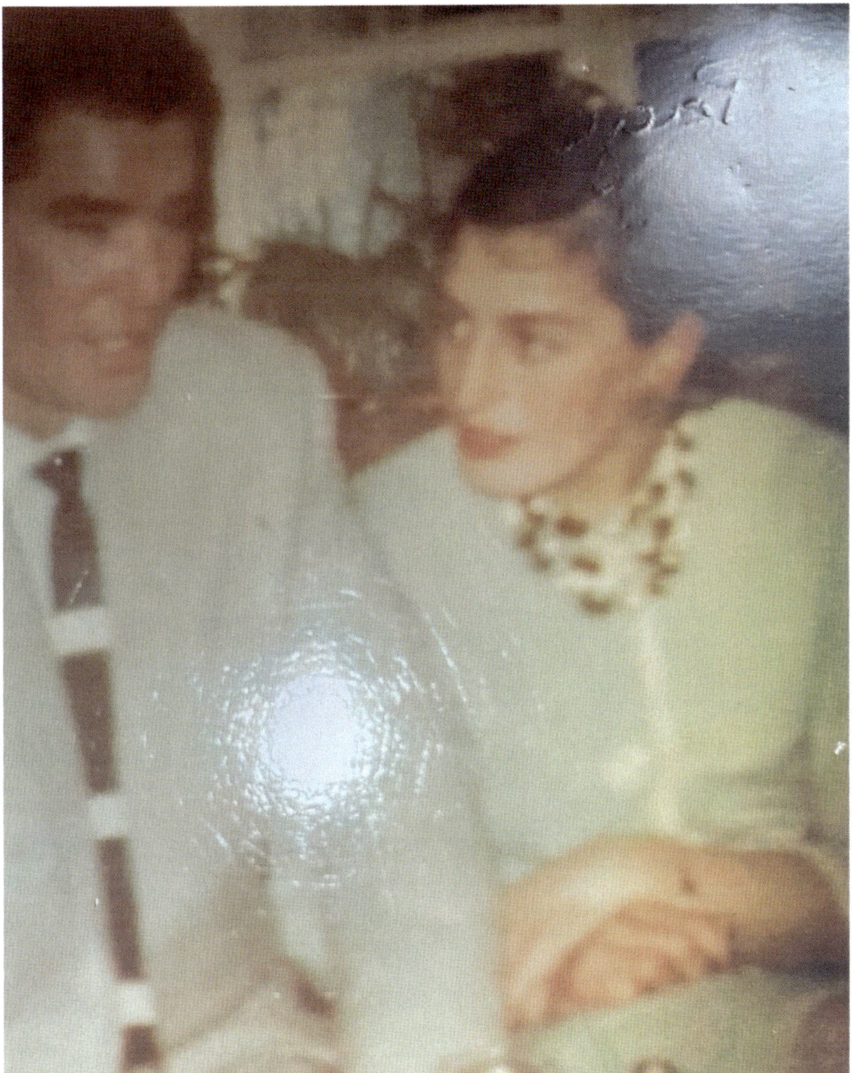

SHALL I BEGIN…………………………….

The winter of 1962 into 1963 hit the records. It was headlined as being the worst winter on record for the UK. With heavy drifting snow over most of the country. It was known as the big freeze. It was so cold that some of the sea froze in places. It was the coldest winter since 1740.

I was just a twinkle in my mother's eye. While she was busy being a full time Mum to my three brothers. My Dad was around at the time. He was occupied with his job as a Tanker driver or sitting in the Merebrook pub with his cronies. They all resided in a council house on Oakfield Road within the growing village of Bromborough. The 1960s was a changing world. Fashions were changing, hem lines becoming shorter. Music was becoming less tame. It was the era of The Beatles, The Who and The Rolling Stones. Young women began screaming for the new bands. Youngsters were experimenting with using drugs and free love. The older generation were stuck in a time warp. Many families still had outside toilets, there was no soft toilet paper only IZAL or paper to wipe their bottoms. The 11 plus was still running. Labour were in power. Harold Wilson was our leader at the time. Old fashioned values were his thing. In 1963 my mum became pregnant with me.

The following year on the 14th of July 1964 in the local maternity hospital called Heathfield Hospital in the early hours I was born. Heathfield Hospital was classed as a maternity home. It was founded in 1948 and was closed in 1976. It was a grand, handsome looking building in beautiful landscaped grounds. It was situated opposite Brotherton Park. When it closed its doors in 1976 it was demolished and a housing estate now sits on its site. My mum boasted about how lovely the gardens were, how nice it was to stroll round them. She told us how you didn't get chucked out in a day or two but you were encouraged to stay there to get fit and healthy to be able to look after your new born baby, before going home to look after the rest of your family. My mum was elated giving birth to a daughter after having three boys. She was given a Cow & Gate card with a pink ribbon which she wrote her thoughts on about what she was feeling at the time. I was taken home to 23 Oakfield Road Bromborough to meet my Dad and my three older brothers.

Notes for Mother

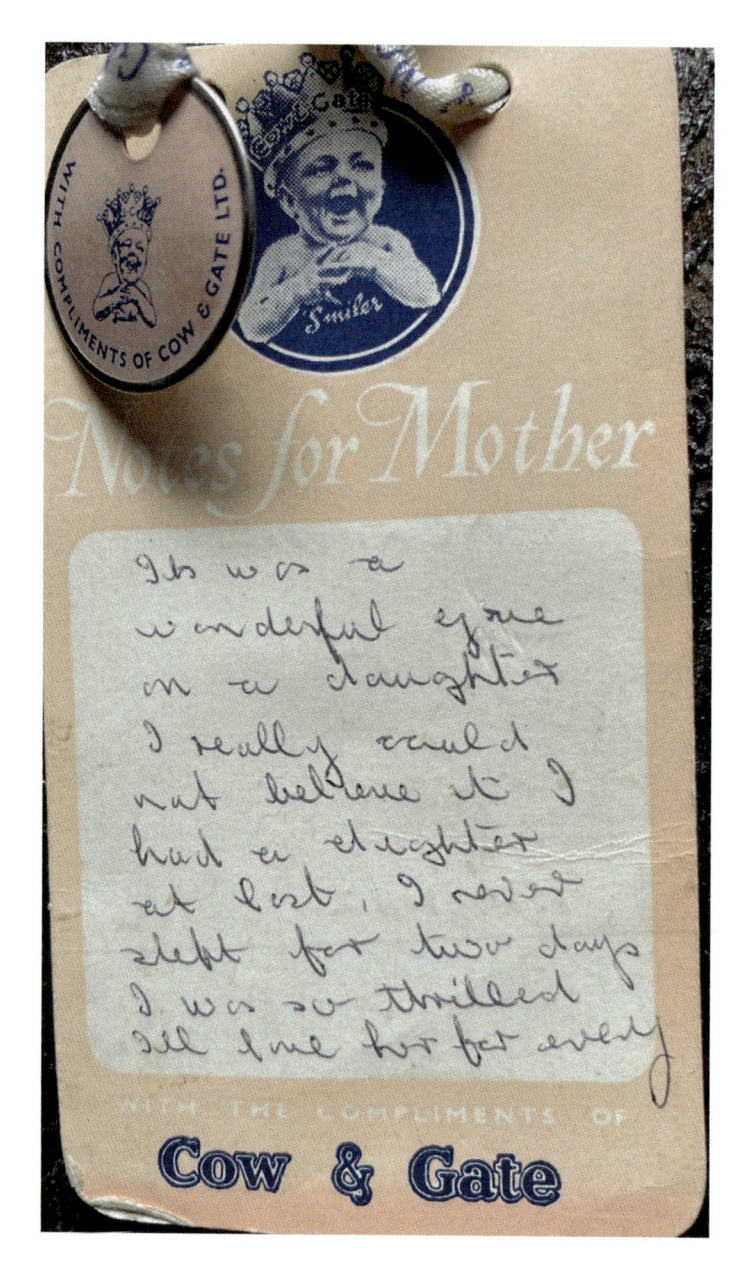

It was a wonderful gone on a daughter I really could not believe it I had a daughter at last, I never slept for two days I was so thrilled till I me to fat every

Cow & Gate

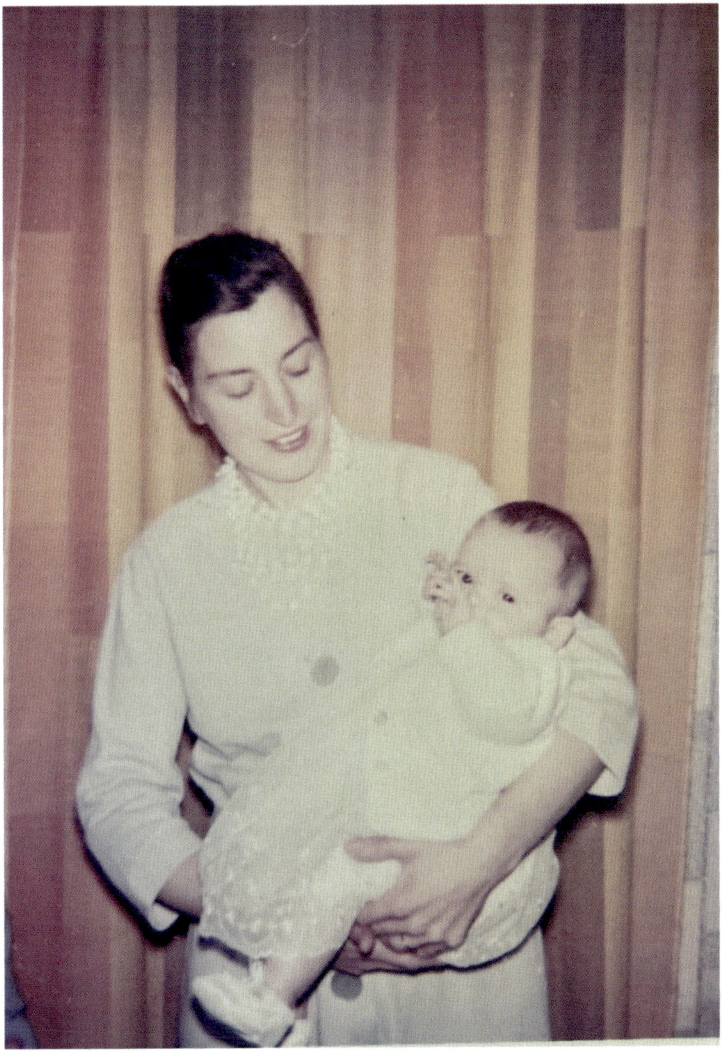

I am fussed over by my three big brothers and spoilt in every way from every direction. When I watch the old cine films that my dad took and the old photos of us all I am in awe of my brothers love for me. All four of us wanted for nothing. We live in a nice home with a big back garden strewn with toys, climbing frames and bikes. We were very lucky to be well looked after and to have what we had for a family of that time era.

It is the mid 60s. My Dad had a huge obsession with Australia. He told us many stories of his time there as a young man. It all began when he was just 17 at which time he was in the Black Watch. He saw an article in a local newspaper advertising for men to go to Australia to become gold miners. He did not hesitate. He left his post in Scotland and travelled to Australia to become a gold miner. This was the beginning of his infatuation for the country.

In 1965 the UK was not doing well culturally or economically. Coupled with the previous bad winters, my dad came up with a plan for his family. He began to fill my mum's head with hopes and dreams of a better life A better future for us all. An amazing opportunity not to be sniffed at. We had a chance to live the dream that most people would never get to do. Our life would be brighter, better, healthier and happier. A future to good to pass by for her and her children.

Between the 1940s and the 1970s an assisted passage to OZ was created. It was a scheme devised by the Australian and UK government to encourage families to migrate there. The scheme was to help populate Australia and to supply workers for the growing economy and industry. Millions of British were travelling to OZ. The doors were opened this scheme was known as the £10 Poms. It was for people aged between 45 and 72. The stipulation was that you had to stay for two years. If you failed to stay for this amount of time. Then you would have to pay for your own fare back to the UK. An exciting time occurred for our family. We became one of those families who seized this opportunity, we took the chance we took advantage of this offer. We became £10 Poms.

In 1966 our family along with many others travelled to Western Australia sailing on the famous Achille Lauro. This ship had been re-vamped, modernised and renamed. It was reinstated in 1966 after it had experienced a previous explosion. The ship had the capacity to hold 1700 persons on board. It boasted three pools two of which were paddling pools. At the age of two I can remember being in the paddling pool on this ship. Sadly, that is all I can recall of the trip to Australia and it is the only memory I have of the ship.

We sailed across oceans and seas stopping off at various ports such as Cape Town Africa.

It must have been very daunting as well as exciting for families to be boarding such a huge ship of this size travelling to the other side of the world, which took almost a hundred days.

I cannot even begin to imagine how scary it must have been for these families. To leave your relatives behind your life, your friends and the only life you had ever known.

We were only allowed to take the basics, our personal belongings. My mum was ordered by my dad to burn all her photographs, later she told me that this was one of her biggest regrets. All she was left with was a handful of pictorial memories.

On arrival in a foreign country you have no family or friends to greet you. Everything is alien to what you have been used to. What lay ahead was the unknown. We were transported to a Hostel known as Graylands, near Fremantle. We are shown to a dwelling were we will be living. Our new home is a Nissan hut. Number 71b and at one point 80a. I only know this as I found my dads valued client card with our address on and as seen on the cine film that I mentioned earlier. Nissan huts were homes of half cylindrical skin of corrugated steel. At each end was a small window, there was a main entrance were the adults sat as the huts were extremely hot. The huts were old but clean and spacious. These were built and used during 1956-1981. The camp was originally used as a military base, later they were re-purposed by the Australian Government to house migrants. The camp was known as Silver City and cost us £12 a week to stay there. This was to be our home for the next two years.

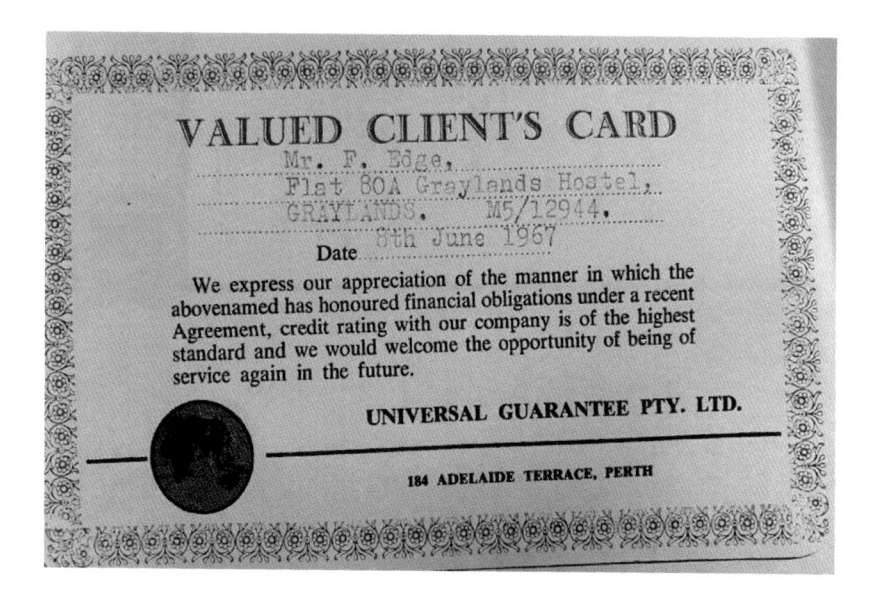

VALUED CLIENT'S CARD

Mr. F. Edge,
Flat 80A Graylands Hostel,
GRAYLANDS. M5/12944.

Date 8th June 1967

We express our appreciation of the manner in which the abovenamed has honoured financial obligations under a recent Agreement, credit rating with our company is of the highest standard and we would welcome the opportunity of being of service again in the future.

UNIVERSAL GUARANTEE PTY. LTD.

184 ADELAIDE TERRACE, PERTH

I have no recollection of my life in Australia. All I have are the stories I was told and some photographs. My mum worked hard in the resident canteen on the camp, working in intense heat she served meals to the families on site. While she worked my eldest brother cared for me as my dad was either looking for a job or propping up a local bar. Whilst working my mum met her life long friend Margaret Bloska who had also emigrated with her family in the pursuit of happiness. Both our families became firm friends. My mum would describe times of hardship, laughter and the unbearable heat. She would tell me how we all got burnt on a day out to the beach when my Dad forgot to pick us up. Mum told me the tales of my Dad and Margaret's husbands drunken nights out. How my dad ended up in Fremantle prison after he had been arrested for domestic abuse on my mum. Tales of how my youngest brother and I got bitten to death by the local bugs. She tells me about how my dad after yet another drunken night in the local boozer along with some other men managed to spend all of their savings on a piece of land. He was so excited to show us what he had bought, explaining to us how we were going to build our dream home. The vacant piece of land that was purchased is still there to this day as it was inhabitable. It was riddled with snakes, spiders and amongst bush land. It turned out that we would be waiting for years for the basic amenities such as electricity and transport. It was miles from any shops and basic facilities. Basically we were never going to be able to live there. Not only that all our savings had gone. I think this must have been the end for my mum as she started to work every hour she could so that she was able to save enough money to take herself and her four children back to England.

In 1968, my mum took us and herself alone on the long arduous journey back to her homeland.

Its 1968. Harold Wilson is still in power, there is a housing crisis going on. Martin Luther King is assassinated. Senator Robert Kennedy is also assassinated. At the age of four I am not aware of what is going on in the world. My major event is that we move into a derelict house known as Tower Lodge.

It is dank, dark, putrid and very cold. I can hear squeaks in the dull light that sifts through the windows. These are my first memories of the time and place of which is the start of my new life.

Tower Lodge was the lodge which had once belonged to The Towers. The Towers was a large estate situated just off Plymyard Avenue which at the time was the county of Cheshire before it changed to Merseyside. There is unfortunately not much history of this area or its buildings. I remember that the road it was on was a dirt track an un-adopted road. It was a very long road that had originally been a toll road in years gone by it was called Pymyard Avenue. On either side of Plymyard Avenue huge houses that were so grand, sat majestic in large grounds with long drives leading up to them. Halfway down the road on the left hand side as if you were walking from Bromborough Train Station there stood a tree lined lane. The trees had grown into a wonderful archway. The branches joined at the top as if they were reaching out to hug each other. The lane was laid with traditional old cobbled stone that felt bumpy beneath my feet. It was quite a long lane that meandered curving gently. At the top of the lane I can see an over grown privit hedge, a broken wrought iron gate hanging off its hinges. Beyond the gate is a single storey dwelling. I suppose you would call it a bungalow. Through the gate is a stone path this leads to a large porch with a broken light and a humongous front door. Around all sides of the house is a huge unruly wild garden. At the side of the house is another entrance not as grand as the front. There are two large windows at the front of the property one at the side and again two at the back. There is another lane at the side running close by this leads up to a local farm known in the area as Coopers Farm. It was a pig Farm.

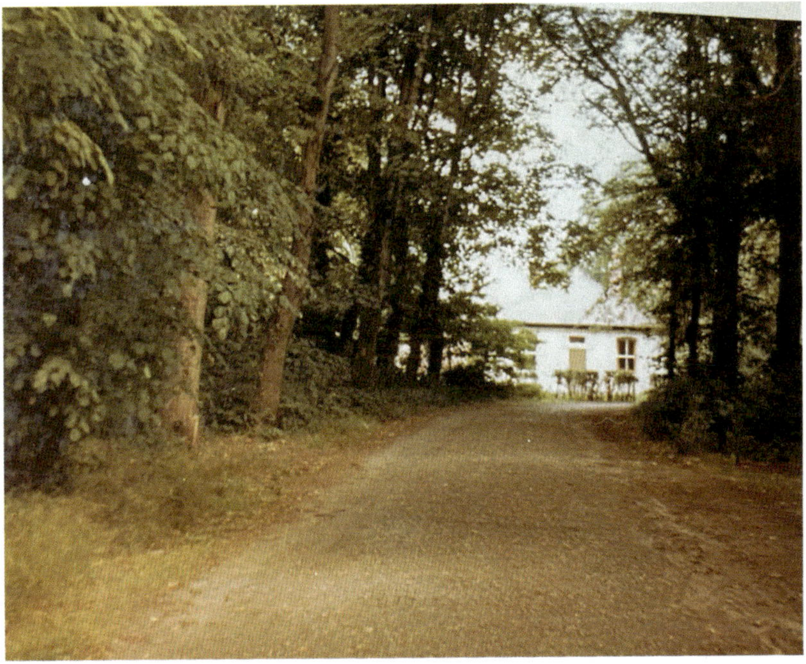

The inside of the house is extremely uninviting, not only is it alive with rats it is also thick with black soot. It is in a very dilapidated state. The lodge consists of three bedrooms, two at the front one large which my three brothers were to sleep and a smaller one which was to be mine. Another large bedroom at the back of the house which I never saw was eventually to be my parents room. There was a small bathroom that had an old enamelled bath, toilet and sink. In the centre of the house was a huge sitting room that became our lounge/diner. At the side of the house was a make shift a kitchen.

The outside was like a jungle the land wrapped its self around the entire house. It had a 1950s car buried and forgotten in the long wild grass. At the back of the house was the original coal bunker and to the side were steps leading to an out house.

Behind the lodge stood a row of cottages that were occupied. To the left of the house was a long winding drive that led to a forgotten sunken garden beside this were buildings, garages, orchards and cottage gardens. The grounds were extensive consisting of many ponds, woodland and fields cascading far and wide. In these grounds stood the most amazing building Plymyard Towers. It towered above you it was vast. At the top of the main part of this building was a look out tower. It had been used in the second world war as a base and a look out point. Now it had been converted into flats. It happened to be the first place to have central heating in this area.

It took my mum days of hard graft to clean our new home to breathe life back into the neglected house. This house was to become my home until I was eleven.

For us as young children it was like heaven on earth. There weren't any other children nearby. We played with each other. The area that surrounded us was a haven for wild life it was home to birds, butterflies, foxes and owls which we could hear in the night. The cottage garden that no one appeared to own or care for grew ripe gooseberries, blackberries and raspberries in large clumps. There was an abundance of them. Raspberries from this memory always makes me think of summer time. I picked them, I ate them with a sprinkle of sugar on top that glistened tantalizing my tongue and tickling my taste buds. The orchards were alive with wasps and bees that swarmed at the rotten fruit that lay beneath the trees nestled in the ground. There were so many fruit trees and we became adept to tree climbing. The orchards provided us with a splendid bundle of fruit as we plucked the apples and pears from the branches carrying them in our up turned jumpers. This was known as scrumping. We would carry our wonderful booty home to mum. Griping pain would be unbearable if you happened to eat the wrong kind of apple, a cooking apple instead of an eating apple. The pain would be relieved with a long sit on the toilet, clutching your stomach. We soon learnt from our mistakes. My mum made an amazing Apple crumble topped with custard. Geese gaggled and hissed as they chased me down the lane when I was sent for half a dozen eggs from Coopers Farm, I couldn't run fast enough clutching the box of eggs. My brothers raided the bird's nests in the surrounding hedgerows. They gently stole the eggs then using a needle from my mums sewing box they punctured a hole into the egg blowing the life out of the still warm egg until it was empty and lifeless. They would display them proudly in a shallow lined box covered by glass. So sad to think of all those baby birds killed before they had a chance of life all for the sake of a hobby. Thankfully it is not allowed today. It was a cruel sport a cruel hobby. I was oblivious to how awful this past time was. Days were endless. They were spent exploring and discovering something new each day. We unearthed an air raid shelter which we turned into our den. We found an old rusty abandoned car that we pretended to drive. We made rope swings which we hung from the trees. We played in the local haystacks at the farm which were totally infested with rats that squealed beneath us as we played. We explored the ponds that were exploding with tadpoles and newts. We captured them in our nets put them into a bucket as we watched them wriggle with life. We would always return them back to their rightful home.

Those tadpoles over time evolved into froglets that became a source of amusement for my oldest brother. He was at the time thirteen. My mum was the proud owner of a twin tub. The twin tub was a machine that she did all her washing in. You had to start off with the cleanest clothes, using her wooden tongs to mix the soapy broth with her OMO washing up powder. After washing the cleanest clothes first, you carried on with the rest of your washing never changing the water. The water would be pretty mucky by the end of your wash but it worked. Once the wash was finished a mangle had to be used to get rid of excess water. Maybe that's why women had washing days as it was literally a long process compared to today. The mangle was outside in the porch. Once the excess water was driven out the clothes using the mangle they were then hung on a long washing line with a prop to push the line up so it would catch the wind hence drying your clothes then eventually finished off by being hung on a maiden depending on the time of year. Much to my disgust, shock and horror I witnessed my brother putting tiny froglets that he had caught that day through the mangle. I am not sure why he did this or what was going through his mind at the time or what possessed him to do such an awful cruel thing.

I was guilty of watching this sadistic display from my brother. I squealed in horror as I watched. Did I try to stop him could I stop him? I don't recall him ever being told off for doing this or being punished for what he did. All I could think was my mum is going to have to clean this before she puts our clothes through the mangle. This is a memory I have never forgotten due to the fact that my eldest brother was always to me such a gentle person and I never knew or found out what possessed him that day to do what he did.

Behind our house lived the Farrells. I saw them briefly I never did find out where they went. There also lived an ancient old lady, who probably wasn't that old but seemed old to me. She had little sprouts of hair on her head. She was almost bald. Her name was Mrs Hislop. Mrs Hislop fed the local rats. She would put scraps of food into a frying pan. She placed the frying pan on top of her corrugated shed roof. I watched her and listened to her talking to the rats. I was scared of her only because she looked a bit like a witch that you see in story books. I would be mesmerised as she stood at her kitchen window washing her lolloping breasts over her kitchen sink. I would wonder to myself would I have breasts like that when I was older. If so I would rather not have any as they were not beautiful in any way. I didn't know this women's life I only knew what I saw and created in my own mind. She never spoke to us. She was a private person. I used to spy on her from our back garden.

We acquired many pets when we moved here. There were two mice that lived in the out house. Those two mice became 200 mice. I don't know what became of them. We had three rabbits who lived on top of the coal bunker in a rabbit hutch. Two where black and white the other was pure white with pink eyes an albino rabbit. We didn't play with them they were never out in the wilderness were they should have been. It was cruel really. I will never know what happened to them or where they disappeared to. We acquired a stray Collie dog for a while who we called Smokey. He would often take himself off to the local Coopers farm returning home with bits of manure stuck in his teeth and a fowl smelling breath. But we all loved him. He once tried to take the leg off the post man and all of a sudden he was gone from our lives. We had a tortoise. His name was Slow Coach his name was painted on his back. Like all our pets they gradually disappeared from our lives with some random excuse. Apparently

Slowcoach took himself off to London. All I could think was its going to take him an awful long time to get there and back. I never saw my tortoise again. We had a budgie called Joey. Our Budgie was blue and white. Didn't everyone have a budgie then called Joey!!!!!! He would live in his small cage looking at himself in the mirror very rarely going out of the cage to fly round or to feel the freedom that he deserved. When he did manage to be allowed out on rare occasions he would leave remnants of sloppy white poo that coated our furniture. He was soon given a new home with my uncle Ronnie. On this occasion I was very pleased that he was given the chance of a better home than we could provide for him. I knew my uncle would give him a better life. He did.

Its still 1968…… The weather always seems to be sunny and warm. It felt like there were no rainy days, probably it wasn't like that at all, as a child it just happened to feel like that. My brothers have me playing a game called split the kipper. This game involves a pen knife which all boys seemed to own one. The knife is flicked by one player into the ground. You as the other player have to place your foot where it lands. The knife is then flicked again. You then have to place your other foot on where it lands. Until eventually you fall over because your legs are so wide apart. It is a bit like the game Twister. I was also regularly talked into being the goalie when they played football. When my brothers started school I spent most of my time sitting in a tree. I loved climbing trees, I enjoyed the feeling of being high off the ground which made me feel safe. I would take a blanket from the house along with a book, the book was always Lowly Worm by Richard Scarry. The busy world books which were created in 1963. I couldn't read but spent many hours looking at the pictures, making up my own stories, while peeling and eating beech nuts that fell from the local trees. I didn't have any friends so I found myself on my own quite a lot. I wasn't a girlie girl. I was more of a tom boy. I didn't do dolls, prams or stuff like that. Although I did have a silver cross pram and a Tiny Tears doll, they stayed in the hall at home while I played out getting scratches, scrapes and dirty knees. I wouldn't say I was lonely I don't remember feeling this emotion at the time.

When at the age of four and a half loomed so did school. It sent its clutches to take me away from my Mummy's arms and the comfort of my home. That very first day I held my mums hand tightly. My new school wasn't far away. The school was a very modern school. There is no historical information about the school. These are my memories from September 1968.

Raeburn Infant/Junior school was a one level building. It had a huge playground. Surrounding it was a mass of wooded grounds which eventually got chopped down much to our dismay due to the fact children arrived back late for class as they were still enjoying themselves playing in the woods. Most of the classrooms within the school were open plan. One part of the building had a special room for some children to sleep in as it contained beds. The Headmaster during my time there was a Mr Barnett, his secretary was a gorgeous old lady with a huge smile and a warm heart. Her name was Mrs Drinkwater. The school consisted of long corridors with a central open air space in the middle which was all glass. There was a massive hall where we attended assembly in the mornings and ate our lunch in there. Other times it was used for special events such as the seasonal school play. If the weather was bad, we had PE in there. At break times the infants were given a mini bottle of milk with a striped straw, this was delivered daily by the chosen milk monitor. The milk was often warm. I never did enjoy it. We were more or less forced to finish it. To this day I detest the taste of milk.

Raeburn School became a big part of my life as I attended the school until I was eleven. It holds so many memories for me in so many ways. As an infant aged four and a half I carried round with me a purse it was plastic with big shiny roses and a gold clasp. Inside the purse was my lipstick, a plastic toy lipstick. I would go to the toilets were I would apply my lipstick just like I had witnessed my mum doing every morning before she left the house. The purse and the lipstick were a source of comfort for me in my first year of school. We didn't have a school uniform, my mum sent me to school in the most beautiful dresses complete with snow white knee length socks and black patent leather shoes. My brother attended the same school although I never did see him there apart from when we were brought together for the annual school photographs. I cannot remember any of my teachers from my time there. In my first few years I learnt to read and write, to tell the time and to tie my laces. Later in the juniors I learnt to count to twenty in French, my times tables, how to add and subtract. I was also taught a small amount of sex education which went completely over my head. I learnt the Lords Prayer off by heart, which we said at the end of assembly each morning after singing hymns such as All Things Bright and Beautiful and We Plough the Fields and Scatter. I was taught to knit by a kindly dinner lady at break times. In the great scheme of things for all the time I attended this school I didn't actually learn very much at all. My favourite time at school was the break times playing all the wonderful games. They were the best memories for me. Surely we can all remember them. Farmers in the den. Queenio, Coko, who's got the ballio? What's the time Mr Wolf. Bull Dog. In and out those darkey Bluebells. Hand clapping games. My mummy told if I was goodie. Skipping games. All in together girls, never mind the weather girls. Hopscotch, leapfrog, Orange and Lemons. Conkers, Jacks, marbles. Cats Cradle. Elastics and tag. Making daisy chains. Playing kiss chase. We brought toys from home into school such as our Yoyos and our Clackers. We practiced our crabs to perfection along with handstands. The list is endless, we had so much to do at break times. It was a time of fun and innocence. There were no mobile phones or I pads or computers. We were just happy children, we knew nothing of the modern life to come. We played out in rain hail and snow. For me personally I am glad I was growing up in that era. After school we would walk home. There were no parents picking us up in cars at the school gates. We arrived home only when it was getting dark or our tummies were rumbling from hunger. Our front door was never locked, if mum was out when I got home I would just watch TV until she got home.

My Dad has returned from Australia. He has returned to our new family home with his tail between his legs. I don't know what he said to my mum, but she took him back. I don't know how I felt at the time. It seems we just accepted him back into our lives. Did he give my mum false promises of change, did he woo her, I don't know, all I knew was that he was in Australia when we returned to England and now he was home! He builds a porch at the side of the house to give my mum more space. He promises to build me a Wendy House. He buys on HP a new cream leather three piece suite. He buys on HP a new colour TV. He buys the most horrendous mustard carpet for the lounge on HP. HP then was hire purchase, you bought things and paid for them monthly gaining interest. By the time you had paid the total amount the items were knackered or you didn't like them anymore. He did appear to be trying. He even cut the grass back in the garden so that we had space to play. He bought my brother a bright orange Chopper and me a beautiful red Raleigh bike with stabilizers. All seems happy and settled in our household. Mum appears to be happy. Life is good. We appear to be a stable family.

My mum decides to start taking driving lessons. She isn't very good. In those days you didn't need to wear a seat belt. We are all allowed in the car when she is taking her lesson. On one particular day on one of her first lessons, the instructor guides her through the basics of driving a car. She crashes badly into a large tree. Luckily we shaken but are not hurt. This is when she decides that driving is not for her. She sticks to walking, cycling or traveling by bus. Eventually she buys herself a little scooter to get her from A to B. I don't recall her having a crash on that.

Its 1969. The first ever test flight for Concorde is conducted in France. Woodstock is big, the first man lands on the moon. 1969 is classed as the most culturally defining year. I have no interest I am almost five. Just a small child in my small world.

My major memory of this year was to haunt me for the rest of my life.

I meandered home from school. It must have been a warm day as I am only wearing a thin jumper, no coat. I have knee length socks that are enveloped by my black shiny patent leather shoes. I am wearing a cream pleated skirt with braces. There was no compulsory uniform or rules of what we had to wear for school. My hair is shoulder length with loose curls that wrap round my face. My fringe is held back by a pretty red slide. To get home from school I would walk alone. I crossed the road and headed into a cul-de-sac. This was a short cut. Arrangements were made with Mrs Wilson who allowed me to cut through her back gate, then go through the garden and through a gap in the fence. I would then walk down the lane to reach my home. This was much easier than having to walk the long way round which was much further. As I approach I can hear raised voices. As I draw closer I recognise the voices of my Mum and Dad. I don't know what they are rowing about, its not late as school is out by three. It could have been a bit later as my mum has the chip pan on the cooker making her lovely home made chips, using lard. I didn't think as I entered through the side door standing silently in our meagre kitchen. My dad is 5ft 10, my mum 5ft 4. He was a big man from memory, not massive, not fat just big. He towered over my mum as she continued to cook the chips. They both looked angry. They didn't appear to see or notice me standing, staring quietly watching in the back ground. "I am going to chuck this over you". He snarled as he glared at the chip pan bubbling in the hot fat. Panic set in my stomach with a twisting pain that gripped me. My mum's eyes were wide with a combination of fear and anger. She picked up the nearest thing to her which happened to be a hammer. I can't think why a hammer would be in the kitchen but it was clearly a big mallet sitting on top of the fridge. He turned and proceeded to pick up the chip pan that was spitting and gurgling with hot fat. He started to move the pan towards my mum. My mum's small hand grasped the hammer, she rose it to my dad's head. I watched horrified at what I was about to witness. I let out a scream as my mum smashed the hammer down on the back of my dad's head. I didn't cry, it was as though everything was frozen in time. The hot crimson blood gushed forth like a geyser, dripping without a sound onto my beautiful cream skirt, spreading like a flood through the material.

I looked up to see my dad place both of his hands onto the back of his head that oozed with redness. He took his large hands that were now full of fresh blood. He smothered my mum's whole face with his blood. Her face was totally red, the blood drying as it settled on her face. Suddenly she looked down realising that I was there. She grabbed my little hand in hers dragging me outside, leaving my dad cursing, smashing up the crockery. She led me away from the house saying over and over that it will all be okay. We walked for a while eventually returning to the house. The house was now quiet, we entered into the mess were my mum calmly cleaned up the kitchen and washed the crusty blood off her face. She quietly continued to make me egg and chips, serving it to me as I sat at the dining table. I only say thank you and ask for Tomato Ketchup. She sits down next to me with a cup of tea. We sit in silence. I was mulling over the situation in my small mind, asking myself where my dad may have gone. Was he in hospital having stitches, was he in the local pub having a pint or two. Finishing my meal, I sit in front of the coloured TV with the cello tape holding in channel 3. I begin to watch my favourite programmes. The Clangers are on, perfect. I curl up on the sofa in oblivion. We didn't speak about what happened that day. We carried on as though nothing had occurred. We waited anxiously for my dad's return. He came home drunk, mumbling under his potent beer breath, finally he goes to bed. For years after this event I would have horrendous nightmares about that time until they faded in time.

We never seem to have visitors to our house. My dad belonged to a family of nine. We have so many aunts, uncles, cousins but they never come here. On rare occasions my uncles would come when there is a domestic going on but apart from that no one really came to visit us. We didn't have any school friends round. We didn't have birthday parties but we did have toys. I didn't think much of it I was content to play with my brothers. If we weren't out playing we would be in the house playing with our fabulous Hornby Train set that was always set up in my brother's bedroom that was complete with stations, tunnels, hills, trees and people. The track skirted round the bedroom under and around the beds. We also had Scalextric tracks with racing cars. We had complete sets of toy soldiers and cars to play with. I loved playing in their room as it was much more interesting than mine was. My room was full of girl's stuff that didn't interest me. I had the dolls from all around the world that were kept in little protective plastic containers. One day I decided to break off all their heads for some reason I never did remember why I did this. We all owned a bike, we were taught how to mend a puncture using a bowl of water to find out where the puncture was and how to use the puncture kit to fix it. Not many kids would know how to do this these days.

It is now 1970 I am six years old. Edward Heath becomes prime minister. The Beatles have split up. Apollo 13 fails to make it to the moon. Jimi Hendrix and Janis Joplin both die of drug overdoses. Music is booming with the Carpenters, Simon and Garfunkel and the Jackson Five. Fashions are changing into Hippie style. I am six, I don't care about all this stuff. All I care about is playing and getting home in time to watch Andy Pandy and Play School to see which window it will be today. I enjoyed watching my favourite character Dougal on the Magic Roundabout. Even watching the test card was good for me as I waited patiently for programmes to return. Life was simplistic for me. Some programmes were in black and white at this time. Some times you had to bang the top of the TV if it happened to be playing up. We didn't have a remote control. We literally had to get up off our fat arses to stand up and walk to the TV to change the channel. There were only three channels to choose from so it was easy. I had my TV time alone before my brothers came home. I didn't have a uniform to get out of and quite often I had the house to myself, which I quite liked. We weren't given snacks between meals, no suppers. Just the odd piece of raw carrot or a piece of rhubarb with a bit of sugar on. We patiently waited for mum to cook our tea. We were always told that if we were still hungry after our meal we were to make ourselves a jam butty!!!!

When we were told to brush our teeth and go to bed that's exactly what we did. We did what we were told and adhered to the rules of the house.

I don't recall the tooth fairy, that never happened when I began to lose my baby teeth. We didn't put our teeth under the pillow and wake up to a nice surprise of a coin in place of where the tooth had been. I was taken for regular check ups at my local dentist based in Woodyear Road. My dentist was Mr Crook. He was a kindly man with horrendous bad breath. I would climb up onto the big chair. I would stare at the aerial view of the Wirral on the ceiling, concentrating on trying to find my house to take my mind off the dreadful noises around me which always scared me. If you were unlucky enough to have to have a tooth extracted, which I was due to have at that moment in time then you knew what was going to happen next. If you were having a tooth taken out, you would be put to sleep for this. You were put to sleep with the use of gas which was an horrific experience. A mask was put over your nose and mouth. The gas released forced you into a deep sleep. I would always have the most awful dreams whilst being under. When you woke up you felt dreadful. I would wake up crying feeling nauseated. It also took a long time to come round from the gas and it caused you to be wobbly on foot. The worst experience ever which put me off dentists for life.

For my youngest brother and I it was a sad state of affairs. The reason being that we had both been given medication when we were younger. The medicine was Tetracycline antibiotics that was often given to treat viruses. This drug given at a young age any age before eight causes discolouration of teeth. Today Tetracycline is not given to under eights as not only does it affect your teeth causing permanent staining of the teeth it can cause enamel hypoplasia which is grooves in the tooth enamel it also affects the bones of young children. We both had ugly green teeth!!!!

On this particular occasion after my traumatic ordeal of having a tooth extraction I find myself sitting on a chair in the local bakery throwing my guts up. I am tonguing my new gap of congealed blood. After my recovery I am given a three penny bit which is burning a hole in my hand. I cannot wait to get to the sweet shop next door. The sweet shop is called KIDS. I could just about reach the counter. My mouth is salivating as I eye the array of sweets on offer. The sweet jars call out to me. Spearmint pips, Bon Bon's, liquorice torpedoes and nut brittle. So difficult to decide. Two ounces of sweets or lots of penny sweets. Traffic light lollipops that last forever. Black Jacks, Fruit Salads. A giant pink bubble gum that you could blow the biggest bubbles ever that attached to your face when they popped. Sweet tobacco, sweet cigarettes. Sherbet fountains, flying saucers that made you burp like crazy afterwards. The giant gob stopper that did what its title suggests. The choice was a hard one. To either pick from the sweet jars or from the penny counter to try and buy as much as I could with my now sweaty coin. I was impatient. to wait. I couldn't wait to get the sugar sweetness in my mouth and to feel it dance on my tongue. This was such a treat for me. I still remember all the adverts for sweets and boxes of chocolates, I can hear the music, I can feel the lure and temptation that they were designed to do. I can remember the words to the TV adverts for the sweets. Sweets and chocolate were such a rare treat for me, we only received them on special occasions or for a reward for being good. Such a treat………..

On certain occasions someone may receive a box of chocolates. Milk Tray, Black Magic or a box of Weekend. They were given them as a gift mainly for a birthday present or at Christmas time. Quality Street were always a favourite of mine. I relished in the shiny tin so decorative and inviting and the equally beautiful wrapped chocolates. I loved the chocolate boxes with the inlay describing details of each chocolate. Oh the difficulty of choosing one chocolate. If you were lucky to be able to choose first you were laughing, if you happened to have lasties you would be left with the ones nobody liked such as the orange creams or strawberry soft centre. I didn't mind any of them. I quite happily ate the ones that no one wanted.

The adverts wowed me as they were like a story that you wanted to be part of like the man going to the ends of the earth in dangerous conditions just to give his women a box of chocolates, he was heaven on the eyes.

We all love a topic though don't we?

What has a hazelnut in every bite? TOPIC and thick milk chocolate for your delight.

Fudge. A finger of fudge is just enough to give your kids a treat. A finger of fudge is just enough until its time to eat.

Milky Bar. The milky bar kid is strong and tough and only the best is good enough.

I was completely wrapped in the adverts, they tempted you, they made you want the product which was the whole purpose of the advertisement. I was hooked. Thank God its Friday for Crunchie.

So 1970 came and went……. It is now 1971 now I am aged 7. This is the year of decimalisation, justified by an aspect of the wider modernisation of Great Britain. It was introduced to simplify the decimal system to benefit people and machines. It is the year that Margaret Thatcher headlined for withdrawing school milk for children over seven. It is the year of innovation and rebirth fuelled by the political and cultural upheaval of the time. I am completely unaware of this at my age. The one memory that sticks out for me at this time is…… My dad wasn't around very much, when he was there unfortunately I am left with memories of sadness. I racked my head to recall some of the rare occasions of happiness of being around him. These are my recollections. He would sit in his armchair, yes he had his own chair that no one dared sit in. He would be watching some of his favourite television programmes such as Benny Hill, Dads Army or On the Buses. He would sit chuckling to himself at the comical sketches. It is at these times that by his side sat a bowl of Mint Imperials. Sometimes if I was quiet and good he would sit me on his knee and sing a couple of songs to me. The first song is an old folk song. I haven't a clue how he got to know the song. "Lemon tree very pretty but the fruit you cannot eat because the fruit that's very pretty is impossible to eat." The second song I am confused over as it is a Sunday school song, a very old song I don't know how he got to know it. My family are not in the slightest bit religious in any way shape or form. We didn't go to Sunday school or church. The song is. "Jesus loves the little children of the world." "They are brown, yellow, black and white." I loved this song as I was aware at the time that around me were children of different colours. Personally I wasn't bothered what colour they were. My parents were racist, I am not sure why, possibly something to do with the era or their family background and bringing up. Racism has been embedded into our nations structure of power, culture, education and identity. If anyone can remember the sitcom Love thy neighbour which was first aired in 1972. It was a typical example of racism which caused much controversy when Britain was coming to terms with mass migration. My Dad loved that sitcom. He often made jokes about coloured people and he would be heard calling dark people Coons and Nig Nogs I am ashamed to say. I would often hear my mum calling Asians Pakkies. Its awful I know. Thankfully although racism is still happening there is a decline of racial prejudice. After the songs I was allowed a Mint Imperial. I would suck and savour every moment. I appreciated the rare times of this form of love from my dad even if it didn't happen very often. I enjoyed those precious moments.

It is now 1972. I am now aged 8. People seem to be going on holiday to Spain. Everyone seems to smoke. There are adverts on the TV to promote smoking. Most families have televisions. Pocket calculators are now on sale. The Duke of Windsor dies. Amazing Grace is number one in the charts. Mullets are becoming fashionable as well as Farrah Fawcett flicks. My youngest brother starts at secondary school Acre Lane. My middle brother also attends the same school and my eldest brother has gone into the army The Cheshire Regiment.

I am bored, I am alone. I decide to experiment. Like most young children I am curious. The scissors my mum uses are lying on the side, shiny and inviting. My fringe is in my eyes, its bugging me. Its in my way and is very annoying. It would save my mum having to take me to the hairdresser's if I sort it out myself. If I just cut a little bit, no one will notice. Picking up the large kitchen scissors that are so heavy, I pull down a chunk of hair. I snip, the hair falls to the floor creating a small mound. I stare in the bathroom mirror. I am aghast. What have I done, its now wonky. If I cut a bit more then I can straighten it. A few trims later I am finally finished at my personal salon. I stare back at my reflection, I want to cry at my dismal attempt, I now have no fringe left!!!! As my mum enters the house I stay quiet with my head down in the hope that she will not notice. "Karen what have you done to yourself?" "Please don't send me to school like this." I beg and plead. "You most certainly will be going to school." "Everyone will laugh at me though." I cry. "Serves you right, I hope you have learnt a lesson." I had learnt a lesson big time. I did go to school keeping my head down for most of the day as children sniggered behind my back. Do we all remember Nitty Nora. Nitty Nora was a Nurse who came to your school to check each child for nits. If you happened to have them you would be immediately sent home with a letter of explanation and lotion for your hair paired with the dreaded nit comb. I sadly had nits. My mum was absolutely horrified. To my mum me having nits meant that I was dirty and unclean. I was promptly sat down. Then the disgusting smelling lotion was applied to my head. The comb was repeatedly dragged through my hair and scalp. I cried out in pain as my mum cried out in repulsion. I was sure that my head was bleeding by the time she had finished. You were not allowed under any circumstances to return to school until your head was clear of these revolting little blighters. My mum got fed up with treating my hair. Without much hesitation I was carted off to the hairdressers. My mum gave the hairdresser strict instructions to cut all of my hair off as she left me to my sentence. I was given short back and sides. I entered the local hairdressers as a girl and came out a boy. I cried like a baby all the way home hiding myself under the hood of my coat. I hated my mum that day and I hated myself. Not only did I resemble a boy but now you could see my big Dumbo ears and along with my green teeth I now felt on that day like the ugliest little girl in the world. I suppose my mum had good reason to do what she did. Thankfully hair does grow back.

We cannot remember every day of our lives or even every year of them. We can recall certain memories that for some reason tend to stick in our minds during our life. This is the memory that seems to stick in my mind. It is now my mums turn to disappear off the scene after yet another domestic. I cannot tell you where she went. All I can tell you is that all of a sudden she wasn't there. My dad is, although in what capacity I am unsure. A van pulls up outside of our house. Men suddenly appear in our house. Items of furniture are being carried out and placed into the van. I was baffled. I am given a colouring book and some crayons, told to be a good girl and to go and play. Money is exchanged. My dad quickly shoves a wad of notes into his trouser pocket. The men swiftly leave and so do we. My dad is taking me to buy new school shoes. My mum would usually take me to Birkenhead Market. She would take me to a stall outside that sold second hand shoes.

There would be masses of shoes piled high on top of each other. Each pair would be tied together by a piece of string. Women would gather and grab wildly hoping to get the best pair of shoes, squabbling over sizes. It was quite an experience to be honest. I showed my dad the stall explaining to him that this was where my mum brought me to by my school shoes. He sneered with disgust. I was literally carted away dragging my heels as my dad transported me to a shoe shop. Not any old shoe shop. It was Clarks. This was where you would have your feet properly measured by the keen sales assistant. I had never been to this shop I had only ever seen it on the TV adverts. Can anyone remember the Clarks advert. "My mum says when I grow up I am going to be a proper little madam." I ended up with the most horrendous sensible shoes I had ever had. I was dreading going to school in them as they were so not trendy and they were so ugly and they were brown. My mum never bought me brown shoes for school. The very next day my Dad threw some items of my clothing into a small case. He was taking me to my Nans for some unknown reason.

My Nan, my mums mum. My Nan had once been a flapper girl. She apparently had also been an amazing swimmer entering and winning competitions. She had also done naked sittings for artists. At some point in her younger life she had been involved with a highfalutin young man. It was thought that he was possibly a doctor. She had a sexual affair with him which in turn led to her conceiving and giving birth to my mum. There was no contraceptive in those days and having a baby out of wed lock was frowned upon. This wealthy man was also married. My nan was paid off to keep the whole affair quiet. In turn she would receive a weekly payment to pay for my mums up keep as obviously she had decided to keep my mum. The allowance was quite substantial and kept them both in almost luxury until my mum reached the age of sixteen. This was the story that my mum told me. She never got to know her real dad. Eventually my nan met a kindly man called Jack who was willing to marry my nan and take on my mum as his own. They went on to have a son. I never did meet my granddad or uncle but my mum regularly told me of tales of happiness. My nan later married a younger man than herself called Wilf. I called him uncle Wilf. My nan was a glamourous woman. Uncle Wilf was entirely the opposite. He was very creepy, he kept girlie mags under the sofa that were not very well hidden. When I went round to visit with my mum I would sit quietly whilst my nan and mum chatted. He would slide his hand along my thigh, nothing was ever said. I found out later that when my mum lived with them he would often try to touch her up. What a creep!!!! Going to my nans house mesmerised me. She had so many things to look at. It was like walking into an antique shop. She resided in a three bedroomed semi detached house in Kendall Close in Bebington. My nan slept in one bedroom my uncle in another and the third bedroom housed my nans numerous collection of shoes. My nan was always turned out beautifully although she didn't go out much accept to the bingo once a week with my mum. Her nails which could only be described as talons as they curled over due to the length of them were always immaculate and painted vibrantly. She would sit in her chair by the fire chain smoking whilst filing her nails. She peed in a bucket at the bottom of the stairs, you could always smell stale urine when you entered the house. Her home was always clean and tidy. She ended up dying when she was 76 from smoking too much! My dad and I arrived at her house that day. My dad rapped hard on the front door as I stood at the gate not knowing what to expect. Uncle Wilf answered the door. "Is she here?" My dad growled. "No she isn't." "We don't know where she is." I could hear my nan in the back ground shouting. "She's not here Frank." Dad shoved me up the garden path throwing my case after me which slid along the mossy pathway. "You have her." Dad boomed. I didn't particularly want to stay with my nan, I wanted my mum. Nan didn't want me either as it turned out. Dad was forced to return home with me in tow. Some time later my mum eventually returns to the family home. There are no explanations. The incident is never discussed. Life returns to a bit of normality until the next time. As there is always a next time. Me I was just happy to have my mum back. This is not the last time that she disappears. Throughout my youth either my mum or dad were frequently going away after a domestic eventually turning up as if nothing had ever happened. At some point after this I was told we were put in a care home for a while but I cannot find evidence of this apart from what my youngest brother told me. I cannot remember being in a care home but sometimes our minds choose to forget things we really don't want to remember.

In 1972 still at the age of 8 I spend my time climbing trees. I ride my beautiful red Raleigh bike without stabilizers, no more crashing into hedges. The seat and handle bars have been risen so that I can get a good few more years out of this bike. My brothers would often send me up to the off licence to get sweets for them and I would receive 10p for going. It was often dark. I would ride up Plymyard Avenue to the off licence at the Merebrook. There were hardly any street lights. Shadows would loom from the surrounding trees and hedges along the way as I peddled like the clappers to get back home.

I did at one point try my hand at a bit of selling. I dragged my old wooden desk onto the cobbles of our lane. Lifting the lid, I placed my freshly picked scented beautiful bluebells. I tied them them together into small bunches with pieces of string, laying them carefully so as not to crush them. I had a small bowl on top to collect my takings. I waited patiently for someone to walk by so I could sell my wares just like on the film My Fair Lady. I waited most of the day. Not one person came by. Disappointed I tossed the Bluebells back into the woods and stormed into the house and lay on my bed feeling sad. I lay thinking maybe I could possibly try selling my perfume that I had made from rose petals and water that was stored in toothbrush containers that were now leaking in my knicker draw. I never did try again. Maybe I am not cut out to be an entrepreneur after all. It was back to the drawing board for me to figure out another way of making some money to buy sweets.

We were lucky children. Every year my mum would take us on an annual holiday. During the summer holidays we would go down to visit my mums friend in Somerset or we would be taken to Rhyl. We would stay at the Robin Hood Camp. As my brothers got older it would end up being only my mum, my nan, my youngest brother and me who would go. The Robin Hood Camp is still there to this day. Rhyl, sadly it has seen better days. It has drastically changed like most seaside resorts up and down the country. We have failed to save our piers and our heritage. Amazing Victorian buildings have been mowed down and replaced with modern box like structures. These will not stand the test of time like the wonderful Victorian designs and the decorative architectural structures of that era.

I adored Rhyl. I loved the sights, the sounds, the smells, the taste of the seaside. I was enthralled with the fairground, its lights, the music and the fast rides. "Scream if you want to go faster." I delighted in the buzz of the holiday atmosphere of candyfloss wrapped round my tongue bringing my taste buds alive. I revelled in the array of rock on sale, sticks of rainbows with the name Rhyl running through the centre. The paper plates of rock egg and bacon lying sticky beneath the plastic cover. My favourite was the giant red sugar dummy which would last for the whole holiday leaving me with a very sore tongue. Holiday makers walked round wearing kiss me quick hats. Everyone appeared to be happy, laughing, generally having fun, good times were had by all. The Robin Hood Camp was home to hundreds of static caravans we would stay in one of these. It was such an exciting time getting ready for bed and to get into your bunk for the night. We would all say goodnight to each other in the dark, falling to sleep listening to the adults chatting over a cup of sweet tea in the low light. I would lie happy and content falling to sleep dreaming of all the fun we had enjoyed that day. During the day time my brother and I would spend most of our time in the amusement arcades, mine sweeping, which is basically going round the machines to see if anyone had left their winnings or maybe an odd coin behind accidentally. We knocked machines to make loose coins fall out. They didn't have alarms on the machines in those days like they have now. My brother was so much better than me at obtaining money. My favourite machine to play on was the one were you put your coin down the chute in time to nudge a coin which in turn forced the coins to fall off the edge and into the silver tray beneath. The noise and the thrill I felt when they dropped, scooping up my winnings excited me. I took great pleasure in playing on the slot machines, pulling the big handle down as hard as I could which took a lot of strength for me. I lived in hope that all the cherries lined up and that I would win. During this time my mum and nan would be glued to the bingo. When I ran out of money I would hang out at the bingo watching over my mum's shoulder as I helped with sliding the shutters across when she happened to have a number that had been called out. The prizes appeared to so exciting at the time, looking back now they were pretty cheap and tacky. In the evenings we would attend the club house to watch the nightly cabarets of singing, dancing and entertainment. We would sit quietly hugging a warm glass of lemonade which we made last the whole night. As the evening came to an end we all have a bag of chips for supper. The chips are wrapped in newspaper with lashings of salt and vinegar. We sucked our fingers when we had finished to get the final last taste. I thank my mum for leaving me with such fond memories for taking me on these holidays and for giving us such happy times I shall always treasure.

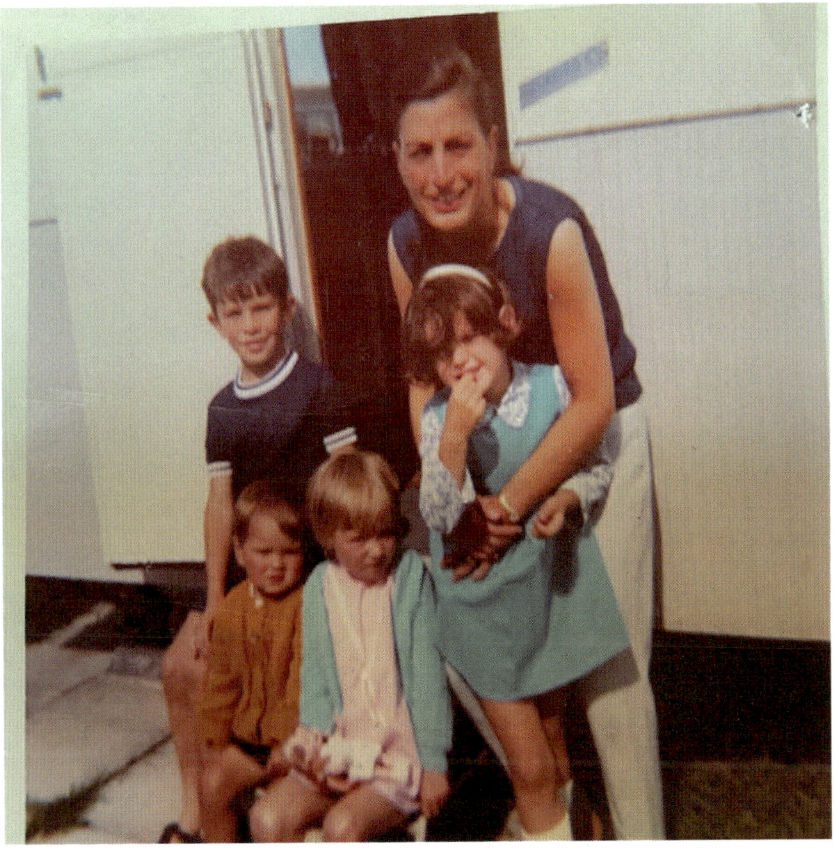

The early seventies were full of hazy days. Shorter dress fashion was trending. My mum always came up trumps were fashion was concerned. She made sure I had the orange hot pants, the patch work mini skirt that buttoned down the front, the short colourful dresses with floaty sleeves. Music of the seventies was having a huge impact taking people out of dark times into happier times impacting fashion and creating spirit of freedom and individuality. I was just beginning to become interested in fashion and music. Lynn Anderson Rose Garden, Al Green Lets stay together, Elton John Rocket Man, Marvin Gaye Lets get it on and The Sweet Ballroom Blitz. Not to mention so many more. In ways I remained still a child as I continued watching Bagpuss, The Wombles, Rhubarb and Custard. I was also a big fan of the Disney films. The Aristocats, Bed knobs and broom sticks. My favourite films of all time has to be Chitty Chitty Bang Bang and The Sound of Music. My world revolved around the television and what I heard on the radio. Of course school was also a big part of my life and the weekends when you could do almost anything you wanted if it was free. Occasionally we were allowed a treat which was money to go to the local baths. On one particular day we were given money to go to the baths. We were excited we were off to the baths. I wore my colourful 70s short dress that my mum had made for me. It was very short with long flared sleeves and three silver button at the neckline. Our local baths is New Ferry open air baths. This baths originally opened in 1932 to provide work, to teach local kids to swim and to provide a healthy life style. New Ferry baths was the largest of its kind. It was an open air baths and was the biggest in Europe. The water that filled it was drawn and filtered from the River Mersey. It was amazing for its era. Later due to Council cuts it was sadly closed in 1981. Unfortunately, like most recreational places that were built at similar times, they were demolished and replaced by housing estates with a strip of grass. Port Sunlight was another one that is now a garden centre. New Brighton, which is now shops and a large car park. How many across the country have disappeared into a distant memory for some and replaced by nothingness. Hoylake and Southport are just two others of the many places this happened. The list up and down the country is endless.

We caught the double decker bus my brother his friends and me. I am eight he is twelve. New Ferry baths was bloody freezing and full of rubbish. As some bunked in over the wall we paid our fee then went through the metal turn style. You got changed as fast as you could due to the coldness then ran through the cleansing foot trough. I could not swim. I learnt the hard way as the boys thought it was funny to chuck me in at the deep end. I thrashed around like a drowning rat, swallowing the rancid water, over dosed with chlorine. Eventually I managed to climb out, shaking I ran to the changing rooms only to find my knickers are missing. I caught the bus home, desperately pulling my dress down as far as a short dress can go. My bum cheeks stuck to the plastic seats. I reach my stop tearing my bum skin as I try to release myself from the seat. My cheeks in more ways than one are burning from embarrassment of the whole episode. A day I shall never forget.

Now let me introduce you to my Uncle Ronnie as he was around a lot in the seventies when my dad wasn't. He was a big burly rugged man. He was also kind, gentle and basically a good man. He would regularly visit our house Tower Lodge bringing letters from my dad when dad would often take himself off to Australia. He would take a seat at our dining table, producing a crumpled piece of paper, reading the contents of the letter to us all. I would sit beside him half listening as I stared at my Uncle's facial features. Uncle Ronnie looked a bit like my dad but my dad was more handsome. I was fascinated by the cysts that dangled down from my uncle's eye lids. I watched his big strong hands smooth the crumpled letter as my mum would stand behind looking over his shoulder reading the words. My Uncle Ronnie tried to support my mum at these times by doing odd jobs around the house. He gifted me with the best present I had ever had by building me the Wendy House that my dad had promised me. The Wendy House became my solitary space that I went to when I needed to get away. I spent many hours sitting in my little place. The Wendy House had a chimney, windows with curtains and a front door. It was painted yellow with pretend bricks printed upon it. It sat in the middle of our garden. I used it for years until it became bedraggled, a bit worse for wear until finally the door fell off. No body would fix it so it became abandoned. It was Uncle Ronnie who took our budgie Joey to live with him and his wife as we didn't seem to look after poor Joey who sat in his cage miserably. I had a soft spot for my Uncle Ronnie.

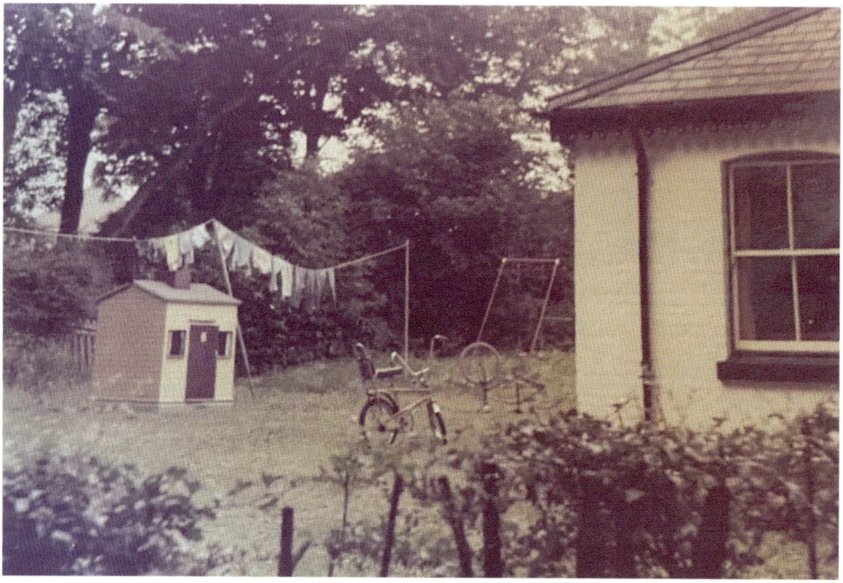

While I was in my infant/junior school Raeburn in the early 70s I found it quite hard to mix with my peers and I was often on my own. Two girls I did use to play with for a bit were Jane and Carol. Jane was so good at gymnastics. She could do somersaults in the school playground. Carol and I would watch in awe of her. It was all going so well, the friendship, until I confided in Jane that I thought Carol had funny knees, of course Jane told Carol what I had said therefore the friendship ended. I even tried going down the avenue of putting my little finger out saying "make friends, make friends, never never break friends." This did not work. I joined in the game of kiss chase. Girls would run screaming in all directions as boys tried to catch them to steal a sneaky kiss. On this day in pure daylight in the middle of the school playground with the whole world watching. Simon Parry instead of kissing me he pulled my knickers down. My whole bottom was there for all to see. My face filled with intense heat. I felt the blood of embarrassment rise up from my neck to my face. I fled from the scene in the direction of the girl's toilets. I locked myself in the cubicle, crying like a baby with my head in my hands as the tears trickled through my fingers. Eventually a kind dinner lady came to find me to coax me out of the toilet. Simon Parry and I were then both escorted to the Head Masters office to explain our actions.

I wonder does Simon Parry laugh about this or remember doing this. I never did understand why he did it only he can answer that.

During the early seventies at home in the early mornings I would sit at my bedroom window. I would listen for the trundle of the milk cart rattling up our lane. I would hear the chink chink of the glass milk bottles as they knocked against each other. Four pints of milk were left on the step in the porch. Three silver top and one gold. As I watched him leave whistling as he went on his way, instantly the Blue Tits would fly down to have their early morning drink of gold top as they pecked a tiny hole in the top of the shiny lid.

Once a week in the afternoons the big Corona truck would arrive parking up outside our gate. I found this time very exciting. The man in the truck would be offering and selling big thick chunky glass bottles of fizzy pop of various delightful flavours. Cream soda Dandelion and Burdock, these were my favourite. Once it was gulped down, drank, the bottles drained of their contents you could return the bottles and get money back for them. Our bottles were washed, rinsed going on to become used to for the home brew which my dad made on a regular basis.

I would watch for the postman to arrive. He would peddle like the clappers up the lane, fling his bike against the hedge. Running up the path as fast as his legs could take him. Then even faster back down slamming the gate behind him as he tried to dodge Smokey our dog from savaging his leg. Smokey was very habitual about attacking our local postman. Inevitably, Smokey was eventually reported for attacking the postman. Smokey quickly disappeared never to be seen again.

Christmas time in the seventies. I found Christmas time to be so enchanting. We would help my mum to unravel the many Christmas decorations. There were the crepe decorations that were a kaleidoscope of colour as they draped from every corner of the ceiling. The shiny stars would dangle from various points. The Christmas tree glistened, the lights dazzled, the chocolates hung from the branches creating a temptation. Our tree and all its decorations came all the way from Australia. I never grew tired of looking at them. It was such a wonderful sight. Christmas adverts started appearing on TV tempting buyers to buy presents for the young and old. The gifts of the latest toys, aftershave for men such a Old Spice or Brut and perfume for the woman in your life. Along with the advertising of what was going to be shown on TV over the Christmas period. How wonderful is Christmas, such a special time of year to spend time with family and friends. Wishing, hoping for snow to descend from the skies so that you could go sledging down Dibbinsdale hill on a bin bag. All the food you could eat, special food that you wouldn't normally be offered through the rest of the year. The Christmas pudding with money in it. The amazing sherry trifle that mum made. The delightful divine treat of sipping a snowball. The sound of the bang as you pulled your cracker hoping to get the present inside. The corny joke and the wearing of your Christmas crown. Left over Turkey for curry the next day or Turkey sandwiches. The day after soup made from the carcass. Pulling the dried wish bone. Of course Christmas would never be Christmas without Quality Street. No school, fire on, heating on, staying in PJS for longer. Cosy, happy, content. I adored Christmas.

This year the excitement is short lived. While being adorned in the beautiful surroundings of Christmas yule tide the door is flung open. My dad is standing in the door way revving himself up for an argument, a fight with mum. We scurry behind the sofa as the domestic gets heated we run to our bedrooms. We can hear the shouts of each parent, the raised voices continue, screams can be heard, we hear the blows of violence, we listen for the lull then the calm of quietness. Christmas came early that year. Our Christmas presents unwrapped are thrown at us by my intoxicated dad. They lay on the floor in a heap. "Have them." He bellows. There before us are the gifts we had asked for. The doll, the Tressy doll with the hair you could make long or short just by turning the key in her back. The patch doll with accessories, the wardrobe to place their clothes inside. I was chuffed as I played quietly with my wonderful presents from Father Christmas. My brother had the action man he had always wanted, Eagle Eye, his eyes moved from side to side. We were made up. We were left to play. Unfortunately, on Christmas day there was nothing to open. Silence engulfed the household. Dad went off to the pub while our mum made us our traditional Christmas dinner. We all sat silently eating Christmas dinner without our dad. Life carried on in its topsy turvy style.

It is during the early seventies that my youngest brother disappears making it to the headlines in the local newspaper. The headline Three boys go missing. Seems that they were all on some kind of adventure instigated by my brother as he was the eldest of the three. Mums and dads are distraught out of their minds with worry. Thankfully, they are eventually found by a local neighbour having spent the night on top of a shop roof. Safely they are reunited with their families. A quote in the local paper from Mr Frank Edge was "I would like to thank everyone who helped with the search and I am so glad to have my son back home."

Meanwhile back at the ranch, my eldest brother has done a runner from the army. He is being hidden in our house. Doing a runner from the army is taken very seriously. The MDS turn up at our home, they arrest my brother and take him back to his regiment, swiftly placing him in jail. My dad came to the rescue he paid the bail for his release from jail as well as from the army. They both return to the homestead. Our house gets broken into, randomly a letter opener is taken, a pack of cards and a pair of my mum's best knickers. The mind boggles, bizarre, odd.

Now it 1973 I am nine years young. I am snooping. Is this what nine olds do? I am not sure. I am intrigued at what goes on in my teenage brothers room. Three beds stand in a row. I can see them now. One by the fire place, one next to the storage heater the last by the wall. It was a large room. It was the largest in the house. The carpet is strewn with the Hornsby Railway lines that weaved in and out of the beds. My eldest brother's bed was the far one next to the storage heater. There I spied with my little eye peeking out from under his mattress was the corner of a magazine. I pulled it out. It had been well thumbed. I began to finger the glossy paper. I just couldn't help myself. I held it loosely in my small hands. I began to curiously flick through the pages. I was perched on the edge of the bed staring aghast. The pages contained images of women, all shapes and sizes. They were posing in different positions, bending over showing their bottoms. Their hands were holding their breasts. They were holding their nipples between their fingers. Some of them were touching themselves down there! They looked so young, they had funny expressions on their faces, their tongues out. They were pouting, some smiling. Their bits down there had hair on them some didn't. Their breasts were all different shapes and sizes. They all appeared to have long flowing hair. Some were partially naked. Some were completely naked. There were girls wearing weird underwear that I had never seen. They all had fancy names. I couldn't quite understand why he would want to look at magazines like this surely there are more interesting things to read and look at? I didn't look like that I was flat as a pancake. The house remained quiet, still no one home. I was growing bored of looking at this magazine. I placed it carefully back into its original place. I did ponder about it I wondered what it was all about. Why did he keep this hidden, the magazine must be naughty otherwise he wouldn't have to hide it. I left the room to go and watch my favourite programme. Opportunity Knocks with Hughie Green. Peters and Lee have won with their song Welcome Home. A year later Lena Zavaroni at the age of ten won for five weeks running with Mama he's making eyes at me. I always remember her as we were the same age. The programme was just like the current day of Britain's Got Talent.

Now it the year of 1974 I am now tens years of age. I am listening to on the radio Billy don't be a hero, Hey Rock and Roll by Shawaddywaddy. I am watching the adverts of the famous Fairy washing up liquid which is like a story in its self. The bra advert. Triumph has the bra for the way you are... whether your ooh whether your ahh Triumph has the bra for the way you are. My youngest brother loved the bra adverts. He could be seen peeping out behind the sofa pretending not to be watching them. I am living the dream eating Spam fritters and a Walnut Whips. I haven't a care in the world.

Dads gone again... To Australia

Mum is carrying on as usual, working, keeping house and trying to look after us all alone.

There is news, big news. The land beside our house is going to be redeveloped. Its going to be built on.

The plans are drawn up. The plans have been passed. Our whole world is about to change. Its about to be turned upside down.

At the age of ten I didn't quite understand the implications of these plans. I didn't understand the impact it would have on peoples lives. How it would change for so many old and young. How drastically the area would change for everyone. I didn't realise how everything was about to change. The effect it would have on the wildlife. But it did have an impact.

Excavation begins. The JCBs roll up by the dozen, bulldozers, trucks, diggers, hundreds of workmen. All the ponds are being drained, the fields are being churned up. The trees were chopped down falling one by one as the birds flew in fright frantically searching for new homes as their nests were destroyed. There was a gradual disappearance of foxes, badgers and owls. The butterflies, bees, moths that had once fluttered over the fields of wild floral fauna faded into a distant memory.

My youngest brother who had spent most of his days chasing butterflies with his net in hand looked on appalled, dismayed by the destruction.

Next to go was the beautiful historical stately home. It had its roots that were attached to its walls ripped away left with a trembling of grief and sadness. The residents who's home it had been for many years were re-homed locally to live the rest of their last years in a strange place. The very kindly old ladies who I used to visit were gone. The place shook, it rumbled, it screamed, it came crashing down to the ground. All that was left was a mound of forgotten rubble that no one appeared to care about. The orchards that I had spent my youth climbing were now no more. The sunken garden within the grounds was filled with earth. All the places, the dens, the hide outs, everything that we had created the places we had fun and happy times now ceased to exist. The houses behind us were crushed into nothingness. All that remained of our lives around us was Tower Lodge, the cobbled tree lined lane that still had the trees that created an arch overhead. My home was almost gone. The devastation was immense, overwhelming. All I had left was a couple of photographs and the memories in my head heart and mind. The area became a place of a forgotten time in days gone by.

When I look back at this memory it is with sadness.

Over the next weeks, months, years, a whole new housing estate grew before our eyes. We were now surrounded by hundreds of houses, new roads, pavements, street lights and this was to become a fascinating playground for us.

Where were we going to live? Tower Lodge was part of the plan to be knocked down. We were offered one of the new houses to rent. My mum was in her element as a new home excited her. Finally, after much deliberation we were given to rent 78 Dearnford

Avenue. This was one of the first semi detached houses to be finished. I shall never forget the day that we moved in. We literally carried our belongings on foot, down the long dirt track road that led to our new home. We moved in and onto our new adventure all the while whilst my dad was in OZ. Tower Lodge was eventually mowed down...sadly nothing was ever built on the land where our house had once stood. All it became was a tiny part of someone's new garden. The cobbled lane still remains to this day. The only difference is that the trees are taller now. The lane leading up to the farm is also gone, as is the farm.

All in the name of progression.

It is now 1975 I am aged eleven. I am residing at 78 Dearnford Avenue. Our house is surrounded by a work site. We watch on the side lines as more and more houses are being built. Slowly new residents filled the houses. Families flocked from far and wide to buy the new properties. They settled into their nests of modern interiors with a front and back garden with a garage to boot. They had the latest technology, double glazing with the latest kitchen designs. They lived in hope of a new start a better world. I became overwhelmed by it all. We had been living in practically rural countryside with no close neighbours it was quiet and unspoilt. Now it was concrete city. The plans for this estate did not include other facilities such as a safe place for children to play like a playground. There were no extra schools opened to accommodate the growth. No more GPs, dentists, shops and so on. Hundreds upon hundreds of homes created, bought, sold to families who were happy to live on a new estate. I was happy that there were new children moving into the area as maybe now I would have a friend. This had been a wish I had wished for all my eleven years. My wish was to come true. A few doors up the same road a family moved in. They were quite a big family with five children, two of which looked to be of a similar age to me. A short time past by when I met one of the children. She was the same age as me, her name was

Veronica, Vrony for short, she had a twin brother called Vinny. We hit it off straight away. She was to become my very best friend, my soul mate for many years to come. We confided in each other we told each other everything. We became inseparable. I will always remember this family with much fondness and many happy memories.

Another family moved in up the road. Their son was a similar age to my youngest brother and they became mates. Life was perfect. We had friends, we had places to play on the work sites. We would often be found jumping from the windows of unfinished houses into the piles of sand below. We raided the work men's huts stealing their tea, coffee, sugar and milk that we used in our pretend houses. We would make pretend furniture out of breeze blocks or spare bricks that had been left about. We would climb in the houses up the rafters as we played hide and seek. We rode our bikes up and down the deserted roads round the estate. We played Kerby. We stayed out most of the day only returning home for dinner.

 At the age of eleven I was soon going to have to leave the comfort of my junior school. As I didn't pass my 11 plus, which I was okay with, I wasn't brains of Britain. I was mediocre, average in most subjects so I never imagined I was ever going to pass the 11 plus. Also exams scared me to death, I didn't deal well in exam situations. I wasn't super intelligent I wasn't stupid either, I suppose I was just in between, with a lot of common sense. It was decided that I was to attend the local Secondary School. All my brothers had gone to Acre Lane Secondary School near Bromborough Village. We now lived closer to Eastham so I would be going to Eastham County Secondary School as also it was in walking distance. The school is now known as South Wirral High. In September 1975 I started Eastham County Secondary School. All I seem to remember is that there were so many students, hundreds, 30 to a class. There were lots of things I had to remember such as what lessons I had to attend, where they were, in which part of the never ending labyrinth of long corridors, stairs and classrooms. I had to be at my registration class in the mornings. All registrations were named after rivers in the UK, I was in Trent H. School uniform was something new for me. It entailed a grey skirt, white polo neck jumper and a navy blue cardigan or jumper. PE was a white polo shirt and navy blue shorts. The school motto was SERVICE BEFORE SELF. It was never explained to me what this meant.

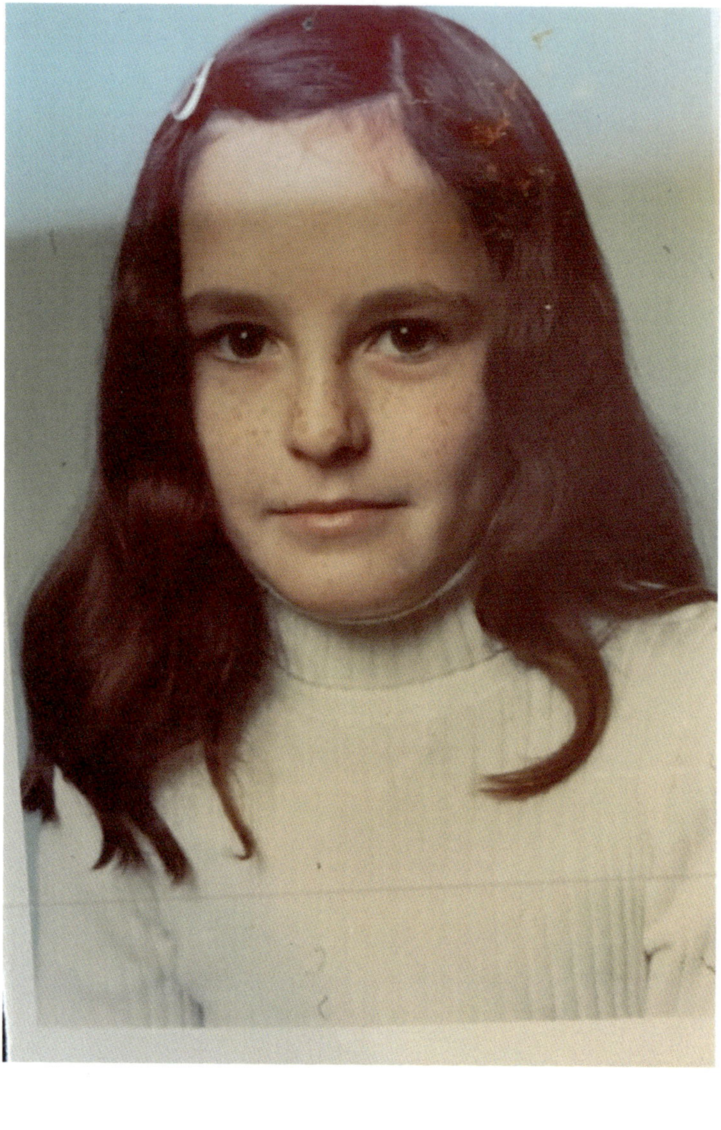

As my family were on a low income I was entitled to free school dinners. I was embarrassed by this at first as our dinner tickets were a different colour to other kids. So the other children knew who were the poor ones. I absolutely loved the school dinners. The Spam fritters, cheese and onion pie, pineapple up side down cake, chocolate sponge with pink custard were some of my favourites. I wasn't into the frog spawn or the Semolina. I always managed to leave a clean plate.

The first friend that I made was a girl who was in most of my sets, her name was Sandra. We sat together at lunch as she was poor like me. She lived on the Mill Park Estate which was where most of the students who attended this school lived.

I didn't love or hate school. I found Maths hard. I loved English, Art, History and Biology. Apart from that I wasn't over excited by any other subjects. Teachers tended to make a difference to how much you enjoyed your subjects. Some of the teachers were harsh, some kind, some a nightmare. I definitely wasn't keen on PE, to be fair it wasn't my thing. The first year at this school is a bit of a haze for me as I had so much going on in my family home life.

In 1975 my dad returns to our family home. He is full of promises of how he will change his ways, no more drinking or staying out late. He provides my mum with house keeping. He begins to do jobs around the house. The first and only job he did was to tile the whole kitchen in the most awful orange and brown tiles a job lot that had fallen off the back of a wagon so to speak. Everything in our house seemed to be orange and brown, until green became trendy. We had a green phone installed in the hall that sat on top of the telephone table next to the yellow pages. Upstairs was a bit different. I had a girlie pink room, my brothers had a typical blue room. My parents room was strictly off limits, so I don't know what colour it was. We had a big garage that mainly housed our freezer and our bikes. We had a lovely back garden that was kept beautiful by my mum. Mum kept the front and back of the house pristine. We basically had all that we needed. Comfort, heat, food on our table, our own rooms to a certain extent. We were cared for to a certain degree. Life seemed good. My older brothers had motor bikes, then later cars, all the usual things that most males are into. They were often messing with mechanics out on the drive. My middle brother had his own idea of fixing things as he would be found using a hammer when his bike or car went wrong. We now lived in a house that was dry not damp like Tower Lodge. We lived in a good area. We had nice neighbours. We where lucky really. All was good in the hood.

We had a back room which was our dining room. In this room was our Sony record player. I can literally hear clearly now the music that was played on it as it wafted through the house. I can hear Engelbert Humperdinck A man without love...Home lovin man sang by Andy Williams. And I love you so by Perry Como. The words moved me, I was in awe of the lyrics. They were so meaningful. I could listen to them over and over. These were being played as my dad tried to woo my mum with this music. These songs bring home wonderful memories to me of happy times. The time that my parents were together. We could finally be a family. We could now share moments of togetherness, love and happiness. Everything was great for a while. Mum was busy knitting Bay City Rollers Tank tops for us and sewing tartan on the bottom of our jeans. She was introducing us to new meals in her updated kitchen. We now tasted the delights of rabbit stew, spare ribs with sweet and sour sauce. Vesta meals and for dessert we had peaches with condensed milk. Dad was finally being a dad he made me a set of stilts. I was thrilled. It was the best thing he had done for me. I would practice daily trying to walk on those stilts. Priding myself for being able to stay on them for so long. Then the pogo stick took its place. Our neighbours must have thought I had gone mad. Our next door neighbours at number 76 were a lovely couple. Mr and Mrs Drew. At the time I thought they were ancient when in fact they were only in their sixties. They were a quiet couple who kept themselves to themselves. They were polite, they only spoke if they were spoken to. They were like most new comers to this estate they were private people. My two eldest brothers at this time were exploring girls. My youngest brother was busy hatching chrysalis in my mum's sideboard amongst her best tablecloths. Life was good.

In 1976 when I was still eleven and on the verge of becoming twelve these are my memories. 1976 is remembered for its long hot summer. It is a historic time. It is remembered for many reasons. It was the hottest summer for 350 years. In London people are frying eggs on the pavements. Hose-pipe bans are being put in place around the country. The tar on the roads is melting! The Sex Pistols had their first UK hit with Anarchy in UK which is quite apt for this time. Harold Wilson has resigned. James Callaghan becomes the new Prime Minister. There are strikes and industrial unrest. Our lives are not yet controlled by technology. Kids are playing out from dawn til dusk only returning home for something to eat or to go to bed. It was the hottest summer that I had ever experienced in my life. My mum and dad are making a last ditch attempt to rescue their marriage. They do this by booking a family holiday to Pontins in Morocco in Africa. It was called Club M'diq Pontins Continental. I didn't know of any children who were lucky enough to be going abroad at such a young age. We boarded the plane in the sweltering heat of the UK, arriving in similar temperatures in Tangiers. We had failed to think and arrange hotel transfers. We ended up having to use the local transport which was a rickety bus loaded with locals, chickens, dirt and dust. We finally arrive at our luxury holiday complex. Its amazing, it has swimming pools, bars, golf, tennis with nightly cabarets. We are full board so there are buffets laden with more food than I have ever seen in my entire life. There are delicacies such as sheep's eyes, food that I was unsure of what it actually was. There was wall to wall sunshine. We even had our own private beach. There were no other children there apart from my brother and I. We swam in the clear waters of the three pools. We played, we explored while my mum relaxed in her lounger with her book bathing in the warm sun. My dad was no where to be seen. The complex was full of holiday makers. They were mainly older couples. There was one family who we would sit with in the evenings. They had a daughter who was eighteen. I ended up hanging out with her. She flirts with all the male staff on the complex, anything in pants to be honest. I am not in the least bit interested in the opposite sex. She does come across as a bit of a sex maniac. One day she tells me that she has arranged for us to meet up with some boys. I don't fully understand what she means but I follow as she leads. She takes me to a part of the camp I have not seen or been to before. She keeps telling me that it will be okay. Like a puppy I follow her until we reach some buildings. She tells me that we are now at the staff quarters. Before us appear two male staff that I recognise. They are both standing there grinning at us. She doesn't hesitate for a moment, she is off as fast as lightening. I am left standing confused by the whole situation. The young man grabs my arm taking me into a room that consists of a number of bunk beds. He promptly pushes me down onto one of the bunks. Now I am feeling scared. He is on top of me thrusting his tongue down my throat. He is fiddling with his trousers. I am now gagging. I did what came naturally to me. I bit down hard on his probing tongue, kicked him between his legs. I jump out of the window running for the hills. I didn't tell anyone what had happened. I didn't talk to the girl about the episode. I stayed clear of her for the rest of our holiday. It proved to be a very eventful holiday. We got to ride on a camel. We attended a traditional local wedding, where I was almost sold off to marry for a carpet shop and some camels. They married extremely young girls off here who really were too young to be married. My brother and I got sun stroke, spending half of our holiday in bed. We never did see our dad for most of the holiday nor did my mum for that matter. Dad spent all of his holiday propping up the bar. We returned to England landing at the airport in blistering heat as the heat wave continued in the UK.

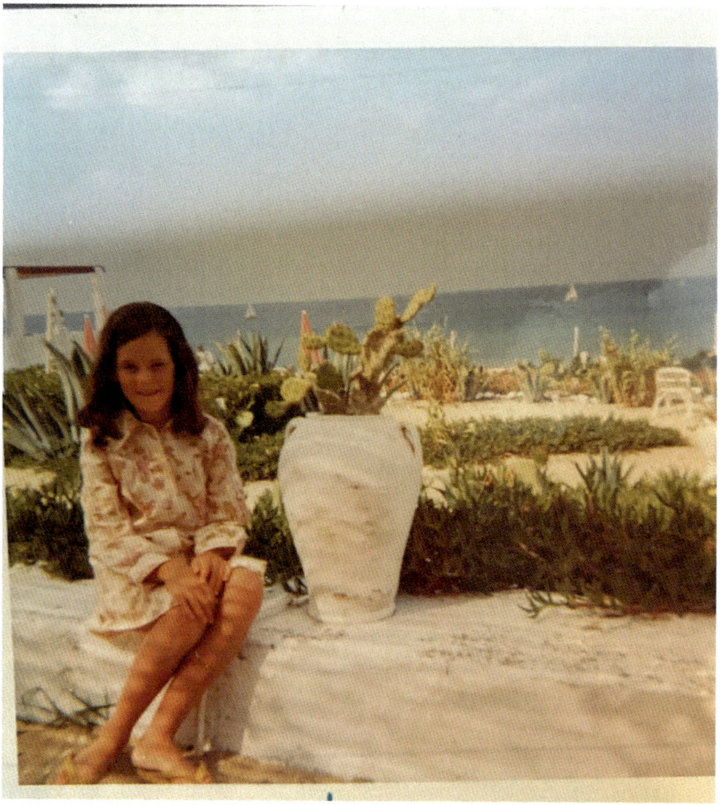

My mum files for divorce, the abuse and domestic violence continues….

For a short while my dad behaves himself as we play happy families one last time.

On one particular night after playing happy families for a few months, the old haunts come back to end this time.

I am sitting in the lounge with my mum. We are watching TV together I cannot remember the programme that was on. My dad arrives home drunk and disorderly. He bursts into the front room where we are sitting. I can't recall what either of them said or even what the argument was about. I remember there was a lot of shouting. I sat stunned into silence from what I was about to witness. I was taken aback at to what was happening. I sat frozen to the spot as I watched my dad punch my mum over and over. He was punching her breasts. He was beating her black and blue. I could take no more. I listened to her screams of pleas for him to stop. She cried out in pain. I could take no more, I ran, I ran to the place I only knew at that point where I might be able to get help. I knocked, I banged frantically on the door of number 76 where Mr and Mrs Drew lived. I am crying, I am rambling, I am a quivering wreck. I am gasping like a wild animal.

"Please help." "Please call the police." They look at each other and proceed to make me a cup of tea and offer me a slice of cake. I am sitting in their sitting room listening to my mum screaming through the adjacent wall. I screamed in pain for my mum. I left abruptly in the knowledge that they were not prepared to do anything about what was happening. I enter the room where the abuse took place. My mum is crying. My dad has left. We are alone. We go to bed in silence, this time my mum sleeps with me with a knife tucked under her pillow. Sleep comes along with the nightmares. According to later medical records my mum suffered from having her fibs broken on both sides.

The episode is not discussed.

I spend most of my time in my bedroom, it is my safe place, nobody bothers me here. I gaze at my pin ups of the dreamy Donny Osmond and the delightful David Cassidy whilst looking into the blue eyes of David Essex. I obtain my posters from my Jackie magazine. I would sit and read the Dear Cathy and Claire articles posted by avid readers. I read the latest pop gossip while I taped the Top 20 on my cassette tape recorder. At this time in my life I was loving the sounds of Abba singing my head off to Fernando. I listened to the Brother Hood of Man, Save all your kisses for me. There was so much variety of fab music about at this time.

After school was out, when I would have the house to myself before the rest of the family arrived I spent that time watching Blue Peter, Crackerjack, Magpie. At the weekends in my PJs I would be catching up on the Multi Coloured Swap Shop.

My eldest brother in his moment of madness had bought a rifle not a pretend one. It was a real life size rifle. I never did find out why he bought this. It was at the time he had ran out of money and he had asked me to try and sell a pair of trousers for him so that he could buy his ten embassy cigarettes that I found it. He instructed me to get the trousers from his wardrobe. That was when I came across the gun. As I went into his wardrobe I found make-up a girlie fur coat that he wore sometimes. My brother was very trendy. He was very into his looks. He was often in the mirror doing his hair. I looked up to my eldest brother. After seeing the contents of his wardrobe I became concerned. I was sure he wasn't gay as he was definitely into girls but on seeing the gun I became worried. Was he keeping a gun because of my dad? I wasn't sure.

My dad would regularly return home after a day of drinking. He would violently attack my mum. He would chuck her out. I would often find my mum in the porch in her nightie. When my dad had fallen into a drunken coma I would frequently sneak down to try to rescue her by sneaking her back in. She would be sitting there in her nightdress, shivering in the cold. I would let her in and hold her hand as we quietly climbed the stairs to my bedroom where she would sleep with me.

In 1976 The Violence & Matrimonial Proceedings Act was created to give new rights, offering civil protection for those at risk of abuse. I can tell you that from my own personal experience that this did not come into play until much later as our family domestic abuse continued. Even when we phoned the police they would rarely intervene. When my mum got chucked out of her home on a regular basis the police had no rights to be able to get her back into her house. My dad was allowed to do what he did without facing any consequences. Wives had no rights. They were stuck. They were reliant on their husbands for money and a roof over their head.

My mum stayed married to my dad for 21 years. When asked why she stayed with him for so long she would always reply. "For my children."

D-DAY was about to arrive.

Dad and mum had yet another domestic. This time it felt different some how. Dad had threatened to shoot my mum. He told us all that by the end of today by 4pm my mum would be dead!!!!

I was reluctant to go to school that day for obvious reasons. My mum tried to reassure me that everything would be okay. I fretted at school all day. I watched the clock. I had no one who I could confide in. I carried a heavy weight in my heart all day. Once the school bell rang, I ran and ran and ran. My mouth was dry, my body trembled, sweat oozed out of every pore. As I reached home the first thing I saw was blood splattered everywhere. The back door glass pane was smashed in. I screamed until my lungs felt as if they might burst. All was quiet. I called for my mum. My mum calmly walked into the kitchen. I hugged her so tight.

There was never any explanation.

 My dad disappeared for a while only to return unexpectedly one evening. He began to bang on the front door while we were watching TV. We held our breaths as we tried to ignore him. He began to bang on the front window. "If you don't let me in I will piss all over the window." We sat rooted to our seats. My mum turned the volume up on the TV, I put my hands over my ears until it all went quiet.

The next day I found him asleep in the garage. When I came home from school he was gone.

He never came back into our home again.

My mum and dad are finally getting legally divorced. I feel an over whelming sense of relief for my mum and for us. He arrives one final time with a woman in tow.

They are both standing on our drive as I arrive home from school that day. The woman is nothing like my mum. The woman is plastered with makeup, bright pink lipstick coats her thick lips. Her hair is dyed almost orange with grey roots. She is dressed in tight fitting clothes, they are very revealing, her boobs are pushed up, protruding out of the top of her blouse. Her skirt has a slit showing part of her thigh. She smiles sweetly at me. My dad has brought a woman to our home to show my mum that he has met someone else. My mum is not swayed as she stands with her head held high. I politely say hello as I walk into the house. My mum quietly shuts the front door on them. They leave arm in arm. We sit in silence watching something random on the television. Its all over…….

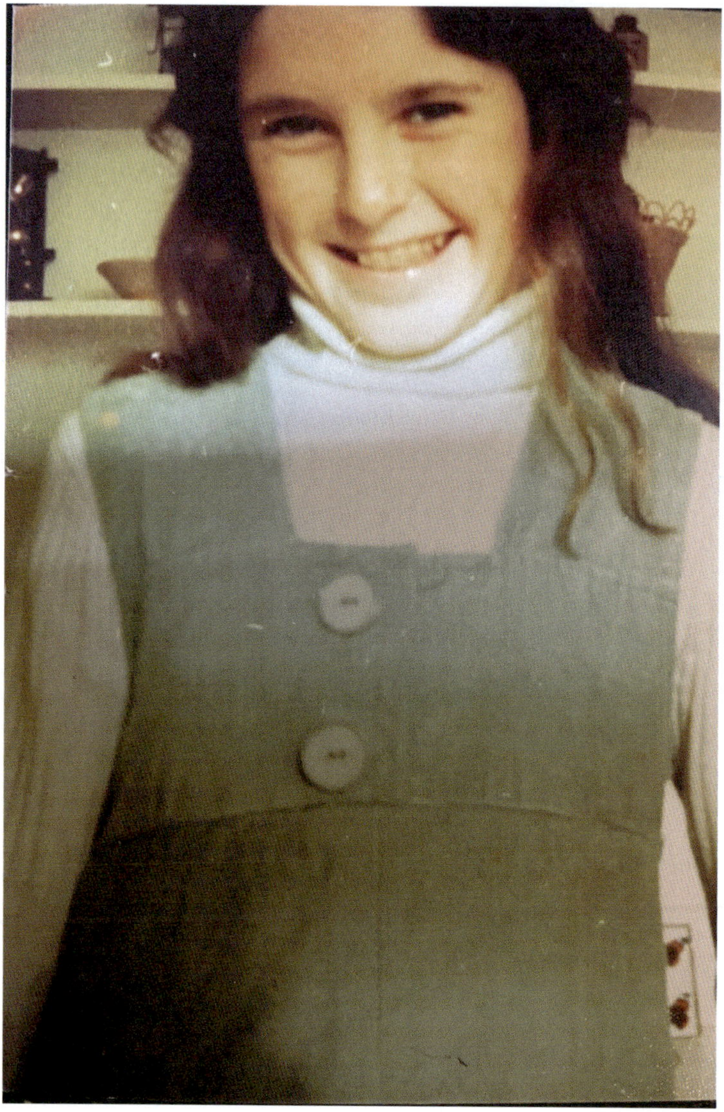

1976 is such a big year for me. I get my first babysitting job. I babysit for the couple down the way. They are a lovely couple with two young children. The girl is three the boy is just a baby. The woman is a fantastic cook working as a caterer. Her husband is a lot older than her but equally as nice. I am chuffed to bits. I will be babysitting most Saturdays getting paid £1. This means I can save. I can buy clothes and sweets. I babysit for them every week and as time goes by I end up spending a lot of time looking after their children, to the point that I am now staying over night. I bath, feed, dress and entertain both children. I put them to bed at night, get them up in the morning and give them breakfast. All for just £1! As time passes by things change when one night they come home very drunk. I was in bed next to the little girl. I could hear them approaching the stairs. The mum went off to her room, all goes quiet. The dad got in to my bed he is beside me. He begins to touch me in places and in ways that were not appropriate. I pushed him away. Luckily he fell asleep. I never did stay over again. I made excuses not to. I didn't tell anyone not even my best friend.

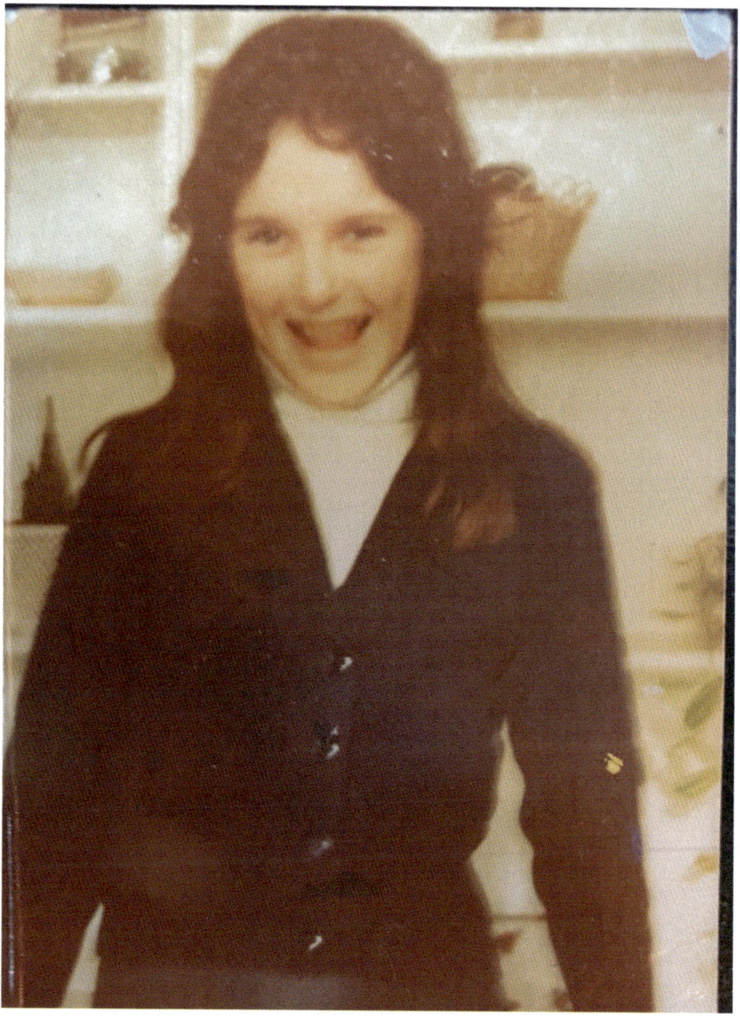

1977 At the age of thirteen. Concorde takes flight. Fleetwood Mac create their LP Rumours. Chips the series airs on TV along with Love Boat. Marc Bolan dies in a car crash. Red Rum wins the Grand National for the third time. Stars Wars is out on the cinemas. The Silver Jubilee is readying itself for a big celebration. I am 13, my youngest brother is 17, my middle brother is 21 and my eldest brother is 23. They are all into fast cars, motorbikes and girls. My mum is leading a new single life, working and going on lots of holidays. She now has a moped, she speeds dangerously down the roads and she is still spitting on her handkerchief to wipe my face with it. YUK!!!! My best friend Vrony and I are practicing songs in front of my mum. She is our audience until we get the local kids in from the neighbourhood. We seat the local children in the garage charging them a 2p entry fee. For their 2p they get to hear us sing, one biscuit and a cup of juice. It all goes well for a time until they get fed up hearing us sing Puppy Love by Donny Osmond too many times. Or maybe it was our singing.

As it's the year of the Silver Jubilee we concentrate on creating a street party for the locals. Vrony and me spend months on the lead up raising money for it by collecting unwanted gifts from neighbours. We then did a weekly raffle presenting the prizes to the winners. We managed to make so much money that we are able to hold a street party for everyone for the Silver Jubilee and there's enough money left over to book a coach for us all to go to Frith Beach for the day. A fantastic day was had by all.

We now have a puppy called Bosley named after Charlies Angels. He is a bit of a tinker. He always managed to find his way to my school, followed by other dogs. My form teacher was not best pleased as this became a daily occurrence. I was asked on regular occasions to take my dog back home. After a while my puppy disappears like so many of our pets. Mum explained to me that Bosley had been stolen. He has been dognapped after being mistaken for an expensive breed of dog. An Old English Sheep dog. I was gutted, I was so naïve to believe all that my mum had told me. In time I forgot all about Bosley as I thought he must be in a much nicer home, having a great dog life. I plod away at school with the few friends that I have. In the break times we would stand around in the playground. We were encouraged to go outside in the playground whatever the weather. In one part of our playground they had swings. I cannot imagine senior students wanting to go on swings now. At the age of thirteen I was a child in those days. I absolutely adored swings. I would always try to get as high as possible, then dare myself to jump off mid swing into the air, hopefully landing on my feet. There were only two swings so if they were taken then we would use the side bars to fling ourselves over. We would use the high supports bars to climb up. On one particular day the swings were taken so I was climbing the high support bars, I crossed my legs to keep myself from slipping down as well as to help myself inch up the pole. To my astonishment on this occasion I could feel a strange sensation through regions of the private kind. The feeling is alien to me but I shudder with delight as it feels very nice indeed. I keep going to continue to obtain this wonderful sensation. I don't want it to stop and I feel my face burn from my secret orgasm. I never ever forgot this day as I realised that you didn't need a partner to achieve it…….

Its 1978 I am aged fourteen. The worlds first test tube baby is born. Ted Bundy the serial killer is finally caught. It's the year of Grease. I still have my original album that was bought for me by friends as a birthday present 46 years ago. It is the year that the first episode of Grange Hill is on TV. The Hulk series is also very popular with young boys. Jaws 2 comes out on the cinemas, it was never as good as the original Jaws. There are many widespread strikes going on as workers demand a pay rise. It is an exciting year in more ways than one.

At school I become a monitor as well as a prefect and I wear my badges with pride. Being a monitor and a prefect meant that if I did something good like helping others or doing good work in class I would go on to receive house points which in turn helped our house team to win. You would then be mentioned in assembly. Also your house would then be up for winning the golden cup. I can't recall our house ever winning while I was at this school. It was an incentive I suppose. I remember at a tender young age of 14 a teacher offered me house points if I would go in the store room with him. Everyone giggled, I blushed. I obviously I never did go into the store room with him. It was difficult to say whether he was winding me up or that he actually thought he would try and chance his

105

arm. I knew of pupils of my age who were having affairs with their teacher.

It is the second to last year of being in secondary school. This was the year you had to make your choice on what options to take. I really wanted to do Woodwork as well as the boy's subjects that were on offer. You couldn't do that back then. I was sort of forced into Hobson's choice. I chose needlework which I was pretty rubbish at to be honest. My mum was very good at needlework. I was given the task of making a blouse. My mum stepped in and saved the day. She made a great blouse that it ended up being put into the school display cabinet for all to see and I was praised for my hard work. All I was good at as far as sewing was concerned was darning a sock. My next option choice was Art. I loved art and to this day still do. I was even given a chance that was only available to a few students. It was an opportunity to attend the art college in Birkenhead. I was over whelmed and honoured to be given this chance. I took History, Biology, English Literature, Maths, English RE and PE which were both compulsory as my other option choices. Life at school was okay, I basically just got on with it. We were all going through the difficult stages of puberty, our bodies growing, our hormones all over the place, boys and girls alike. I didn't really go round with other students much during this time. I tried to keep myself to myself. Sandra who was supposed to be my best friend decided she thought it was funny to put chewing gum into my long hair as we queued for lunch. Staff came over to see what all my fuss was about. They proceeded to cut big chunks out of my hair. I was mortified. During this year at school I begin to be bullied by my peers. I never knew why. One day I was followed home from school by a big group of girls, most of whom I knew. They decide to start pushing me, hitting me and calling me names. Thankfully a passer by shouted for them to leave me alone. "I will call the police if you don't leave the girl alone." They all scarpered. I was pushed around in the cloakrooms in the mornings. I ended up losing my rag and attacked one of the girls, leaving her with a bleeding neck that left her with scars. I began to keep away from my peers. I am being called Stinky Edge. I begin to become isolated, I am left alone. I am okay with this as its easier for me to be on my own rather than deal with any confrontation. Girls are bitches I have learnt.

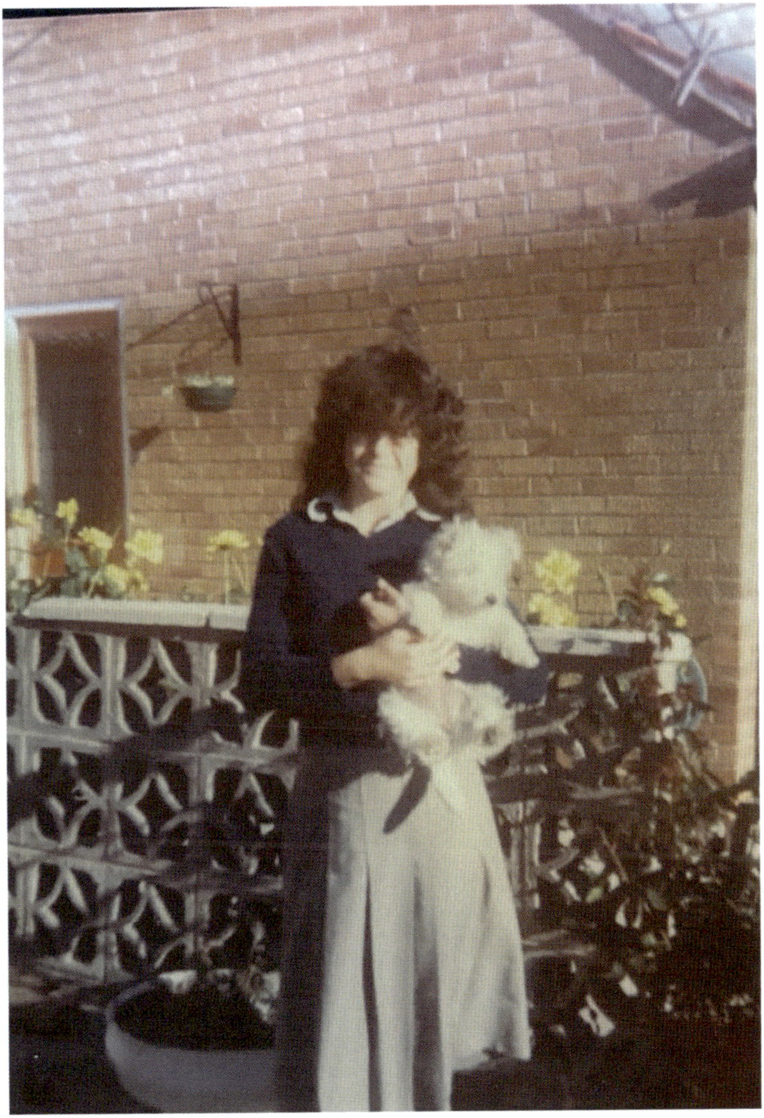

This is the year of noticing boys!!!! I have literally fallen head over heals in love with Chrissy Igo, he doesn't know this, he doesn't go to our school. I first set eyes on him at our local Youth Club in Eastham. My friend Vrony and I would frequent this youth club for a bit of eye candy. We go to the discos to dance and played table tennis. On this night I am going there with my friend Vrony. It is snowing very heavily. The roads are like iced cakes. The trees are icy with snow caps. We are heading there as we walk there along Pymyard Avenue. It's a long walk to the youth club. I convince myself that this will be the night that I get to kiss him. I have never been kissed before. I am excited at the prospect. This is when much to my friend's dismay, although she is laughing as I practice my kissing techniques on a nearby tree. I ask Vrony if I am doing it right as I snog the tree. We are now wetting ourselves with laughter at the thought that I am actually doing this. I never did get to kiss Chrissy Igo at the youth club. I was saddened at this but quickly and swiftly I set my sights on another. David Edwards. He was gorgeous, blonde, handsome and sweet. He asked me out while I was in school. We managed two whole weeks of being girlfriend and boyfriend. In those two weeks I didn't even see him. We didn't manage a date or even a fleeting kiss. In those two weeks I was off school with the dreaded flu. When I finally recovered and returned to school he chucked me!!!!

This was also the time of wanting to belong to a group of people, everyone belonged to a group. The book worms, the educated, the snobs, the drop outs and so on. I was easily persuaded. I was sadly desperate to have some sort of belonging to something. I was always on my own due to the bullying. So when a girl said come with us like a fool I went. At lunch times pupils were allowed to leave the school premises. I followed like a lamb to my slaughter. I just wanted to belong to someone or something. It was a time of experimenting. It has to be one of the saddest days of my young life. I would and do regret this moment for ever. I was never going to belong. I placed myself in a situation that to this day I wished I had been strong enough to have walked away. I didn't, I went along with things trying to make myself popular with others. I put myself in an awkward scenario. This buggered up the rest of my life. Yes. I took my first puff of a cigarette, trying to look and be cool. I coughed my guts up, I felt sick, I felt light headed. Unfortunately for me I carried on thinking that I looked good amongst the people who didn't actually care about me. From there I was hooked. I was in a group who went behind the shops for a sly smoke. It actually felt good to be naughty, to do something that should not be done, that you shouldn't be doing. You could get caught, you may get into trouble. I started to smoke on a regular basis. Embassy No1, Silk cut, Consulate and heavens forbid Woodbines if you were desperate. I was hooked. I have to own up to stealing a few cigarettes from my mum who was a smoker at this time. My mum smoked until she got pneumonia that forced her to give up this filthy habit in her fifties. I carried on thinking I was so cool. I thought that I looked good, I thought I was being grown up. I wasn't in all cases. I regret this time. I went on to experience sex, drugs and rock and roll. Not the sex actually....

This is the same year that my mum takes us to Middleton Towers in Morecombe. I am allowed to take my best friend Veronica. We were so excited as it felt like such a grown up holiday. We are even going to have our own chalet. We pack our cases. We pack our best clothes. I am packing my favourite hacking jacket, my winkle picker high heeled shoes. My gypsy skirts and tops. My friend packs 14 pairs of knickers, don't ask me why I hadn't a clue but this became a standing joke for us as friends. Middleton Towers is quite famous in its own right. It was the first camp on the North West Coast. It was first opened in 1939. It had everything about it that stood for a traditional British Summer Holiday. It was the largest Pontins Site. It had chalets, an entertainment centre. It had a boating lake, pub, crazy golf and arcades. The main entertainment centre was based on the SS Berengaria. It was a sixty five acre camp site that was opened by Harry Kamilya who was a Blackpool business man. The second world war changed the future of this camp so Pontins bought it in 1964. To give you the scale of this site, the communal dining hall seated 3,000. It was humongous. At times due to the size of this camp we couldn't find our own chalet. At 14 this felt amazing for us that we had our own chalet and that my mum generally left us to our own devices. We would go to the Saturday Night Fever dancing classes in the morning then spend the rest of the day getting ready for the evening to go to the local night club. We were never ever asked for ID. We would dance the night away to music played by the DJ. We would then suffer badly from severe leg cramps during the night from all our dancing. I fell in love instantly with a Blue Coat.

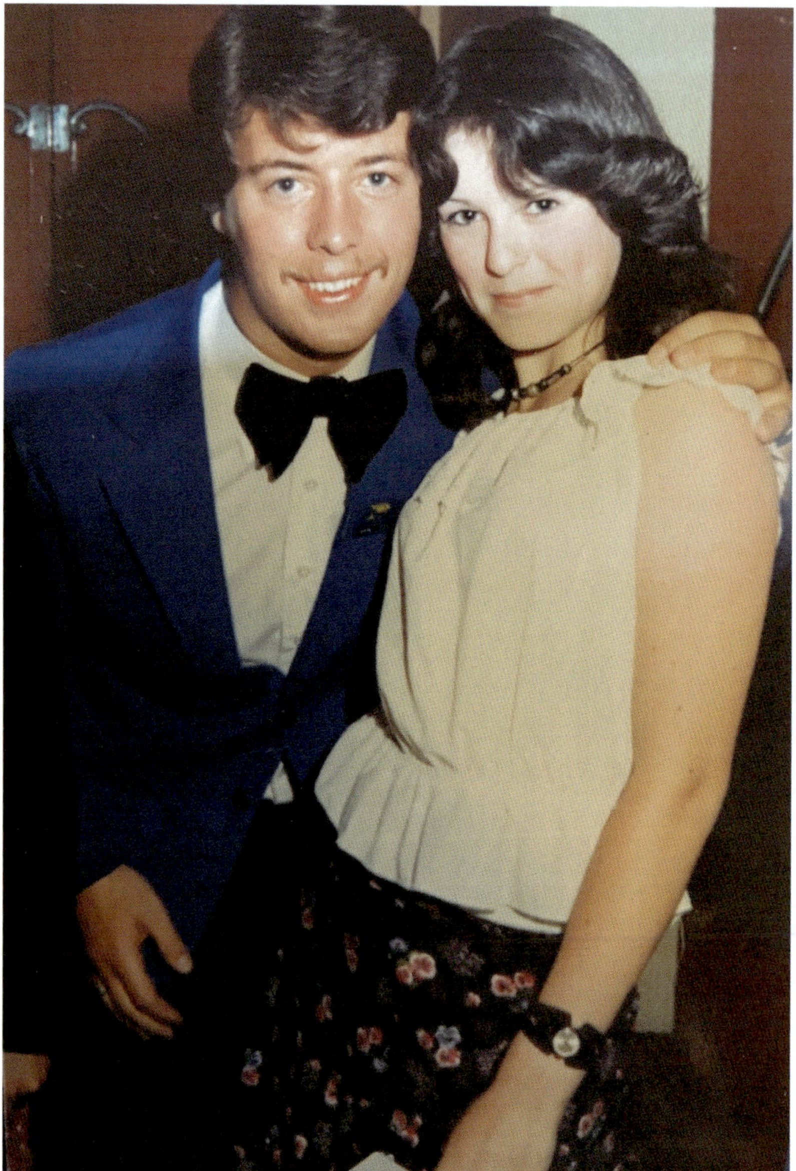

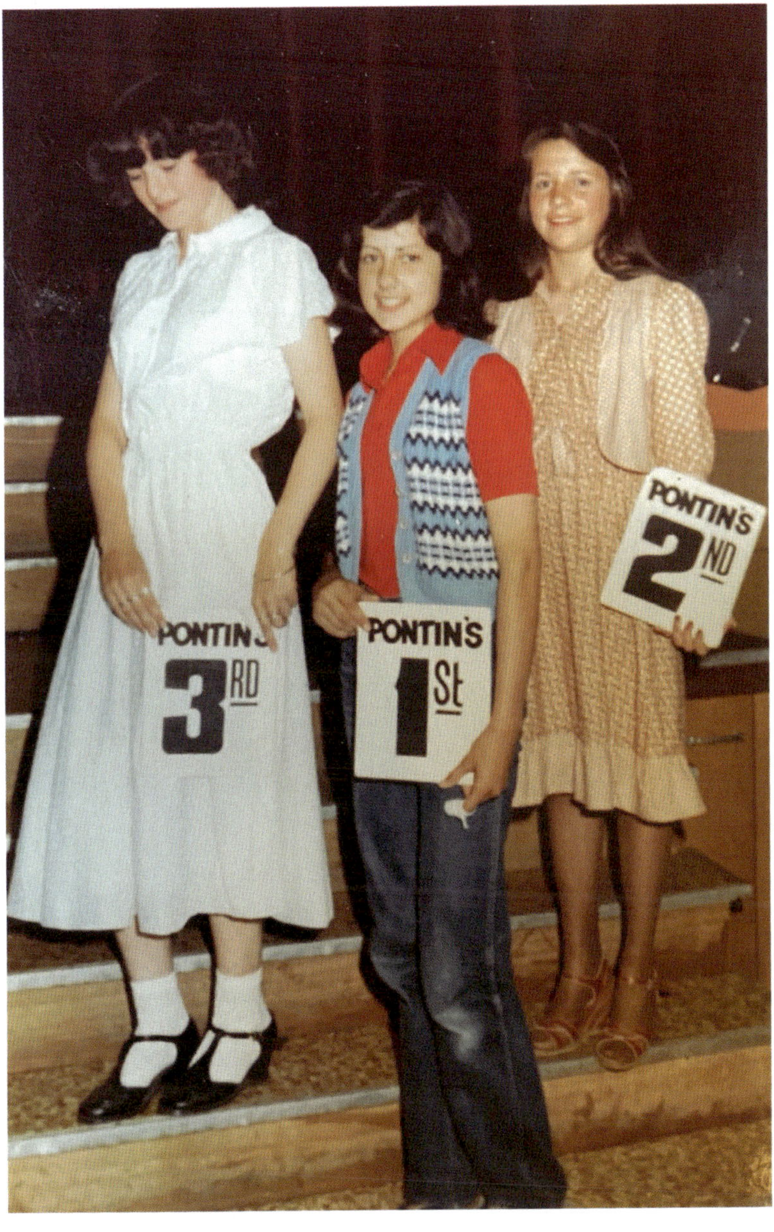
PONTIN'S
3RD
PONTIN'S
1St
PONTIN'S
2ND

We desperately wanted to return to Middleton Towers. So for the second year running we went. This time we return with my nan and mum. This time for me was so very different. The camp was as I had remembered from the year before. Now it is 1979 I am now fifteen as is my friend Vrony. We are now grown up for goodness sake!!! We are almost adults aren't we????? This time my mum and nan talk me into entering Miss Pontins 1979. I am pushed up onto the stage, egged on by my mum and nan. Standing on the stage with judges was quite disconcerting. My mum and nan are whispering in the background. "For Gods sake smile." I couldn't and wouldn't smile as I had green teeth! After all the excitement I did come third. I was pleased with that. My mum and nan had other ideas. "You could have come first if only you had just smiled." I left it with them. Vrony and me tended to spend most of our holiday loitering around the arcades dressed up to the nines trying to look cool. This was where it was at wasn't it???? We ogled at the arcade attendants. Their names where Vick and Dean. We spent the day eying them up as we pretended to be on the machines. We would constantly go up to them to ask for change so that we could get to speak to them. Early in the evening we would sit in our chalet with our curlers in our hair in the hope of having the perfect flick out hair. We often missed the evening meal in the residents canteen just so we could take our time getting ready for the night. We would make our grand entrance into the night club thinking we looked the bees knees. We spent our night dancing our socks off to our favourite songs of this period which were, Silly Games and You can ring my bell. On the way back to our chalet I vividly remember Vick the arcade attendant calling to me. He asked me to go for a walk with him. I let my friend walk back to the chalet alone. I was extremely flattered that this man in his 30s was interested in me just a girl. How green I was, how naïve. I stupidly went along with him. He was tall he was dark and handsome in my eyes. What could be the worse that could happen? He walked slowly. He took me to a dark place. I couldn't really see very much. He bent to kiss me. I had never experienced a kiss from a man. He took my small hand and guided my hand to what was about to be a massive shock to me. I felt this hot, hard thing that was long and fleshy. This thing was placed in my hand. I was mesmerised, scared and confused. He pushed my head down towards this thing. He ordered me to open my mouth. Something inside of me told me that this was wrong. I pushed him away. I stumbled in the darkness then found my footing and ran as fast as my legs could go. I ran towards our chalet, gasping as I crashed into the door, clawing at the lock. I poured my experience out to my friend Vrony. We steered clear of the arcades after this escapade. The week ended as it had began with dancing and going to bed.

I was still whole thank goodness. I was still me.

We never did go back to Middleton Towers Pontins. Again it is now a housing estate. I have fond memories of such wonderful holidays there. They will stay with me all my life.

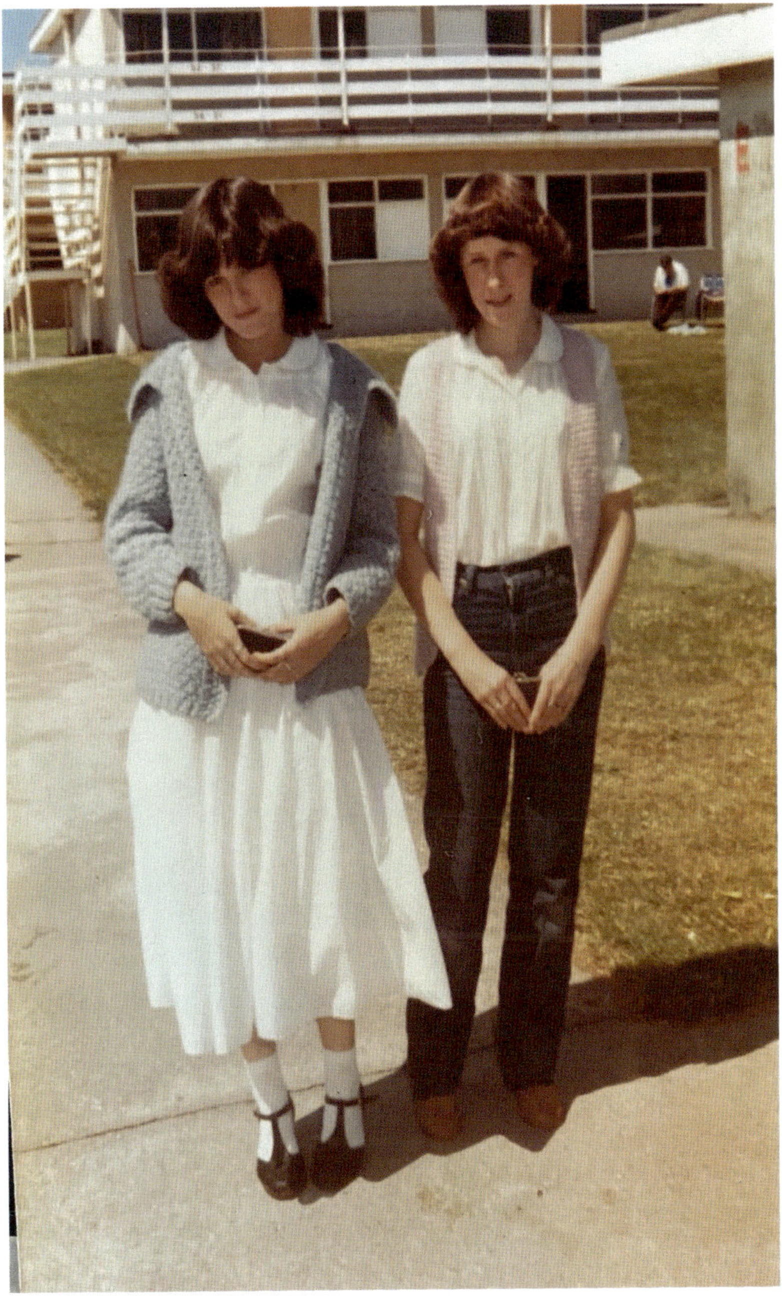

1979 was a big year for me in so many ways. One not to be ever forgotten.

During the year of 1979 I reacquaint myself with my dad. I meet him once a week at his local pub the Argyle and Sutherland. He always sat in the corner on his stool surrounded by some like minded mates so I always knew where to find him. He would buy me a fresh orange. We would have a catch up for about an hour. I would be given £1 to go and treat myself.

My mum is now working at Harry's Fish and Chip shop on Plymyard Avenue. It is the new local Chippy. It sells Chinese and English food. My mum worked mainly evenings along side her best friend Vi. I would pop in sometimes to get a free bag of chips loaded with salt and vinegar. Mum would return home late with left over fish cakes for us. We looked forward to seeing her and receiving our bag of lukewarm fish cake and crispy bits of chips. I didn't really like to cuddle her as she always smelt of chip fat. I preferred it when she had been working at the Dibbinsdale Hotel. Then she didn't smell so bad and she would bring stolen after eight mint chocolates for us.

It's a big year for growth. In school the two PE teachers Miss Hardy and Miss Gray who everyone said they were lesbians would order us to get in the showers after our lesson. I hated the school showers, they were so cold and the changing rooms were even colder. All the girls would check each other out as they ran naked into the showers. I laugh inside as I remember a girls stuffing falling out of her bra as she dressed. I was in awe of the girl with the orange pubic hair. On one particular day I was pulled aside by my PE teachers after our lesson. They begin to advise me that I need to ditch the vest and invest in a decent bra. I am mortified, blushing and nodding in acknowledgement. At the end of this school day I go immediately to my best friend Veronica's house to tell her what had happened in my PE lesson. She kindly gives me one of her bras. I didn't fit into the bra as it was too small for me. I was too scared to ask my mum for one.

This is the year that I think I am dying. I am standing on the landing. I can feel something warm and wet trickling down my thighs. As I look down I see bright crimson blood. I am now screaming. "Mum I am dying." My mum calmly starts to shred an old sheet. She hands me a wad. "Put that into your knickers." "Remember you can have babies now." Once again I reach out to my best friend Vrony. She explains everything to me as she hands me some sanitary towels.

All of a sudden I am turning into a woman more or less over night. I am scared.

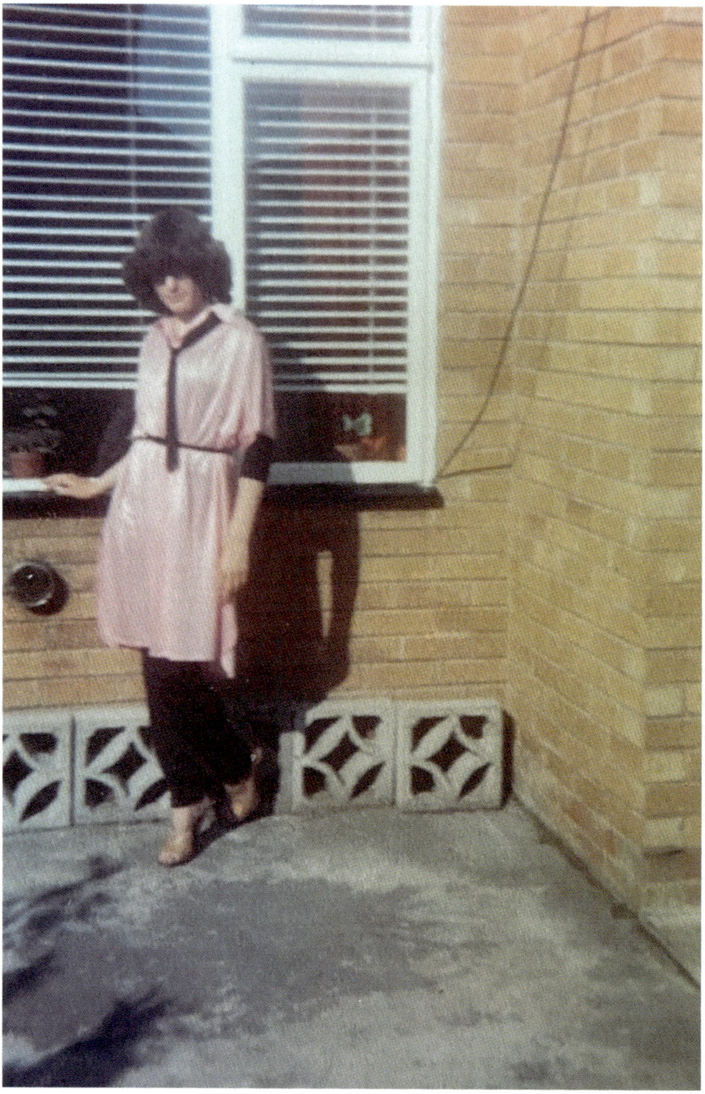

I the year of 1979 Margaret Thatcher becomes the first female Prime Minister. The government struggle with inflation, strikes, unemployment as well as migrants from the commonwealth are arriving. Vandalism is on the rise as well as football hooliganism. Mcdonald's introduce Happy Meals.

All I am interested in at this age of fifteen is the latest fashion trends, catching up with the series Dallas and wanting to look like one of the actresses in Charlie's Angels or the Cadbury Flake girl. I listen and play vinyl which includes the Bee Gees and Earth Wind and Fire. I am also trying to come to terms with the situation of boys who are now looking at me in a different light as they start to comment on my new breasts.

This is the year that my friend Vrony and I manage to get false IDs to enable us to get into the popular night club in Neston, Leighton Court. Ruperts and St James in Birkenhead. We dance around our handbags in smoky surroundings as we sip orange juice getting drunk on the atmosphere. We danced into the early hours until we dropped. We ended up with sore legs and blistered feet as we walked home to Bromborough because we couldn't afford a taxi home. My mum never once questioned where I had been all night.

It is the year of the sore head. My head was sore from sleeping all night in curlers. I would spend hours in the morning to obtain the perfect wings before leaving for school.

It is the year that I am now paying into the Littlewoods catalogue to be able to buy the latest clothes. By the time you had paid off the debt that you had created you didn't wear them anymore or you had worn them to death.

This is the year that I fall into a group of friends outside of school. There was 18 of us in total. We have weekly parties at peoples houses while the parents are out. We create a secret den called the peezies. Its just a shed in one of our friend's garden but it was our place. We discover alcohol, kissing, fondling and going out with each other then swapping and going out with another. We mess with Ouija boards. We have fun cycling down to Eastham Ferry. We collect Magic Mushrooms from the local golf course that we eat raw or make Mushroom tea. Magic Mushrooms have hallucinogenic compounds that make you giggly, excited, paranoid, anxious, overwhelmed, euphoric. Not to be taken if you are in a low mood as they can make your mood worse. They have been around for centuries, taken for fun. They were discovered in Mexico in 1956 and the rest is history. I loved my new friends. We had so much fun times exploring, learning about life, love and a lot of self discovery. It was all happening. These times are one of my fondest memories of my youth.

It is also the year for sex education. As my mum went away on holiday a lot with her latest boyfriend, we were often left to our own devices. We were left to care for ourselves at an age were we were expected to do so. My youngest brother on one occasion decided it was a great idea to hold a mass orgy. All I could see as I made my way to the kitchen was swirling smoke, naked bodies, legs entwined and a lot of moaning and groaning going on. I sort of guessed what they were all doing. It is precisely at this time that my brother introduces me to joints, hot knives and blow backs. I am forced not to tell my mum about the orgy or he will in turn inform her about me taking drugs. The drugs make you laugh uncontrollably, then they made me sleep and went on to give me the munchies. I am not particularly interested in continuing taking drugs they didn't do much for me thank goodness. Were as my brother decided to experiment further with drug taking. He was taking Acid tablets along with other substances and pills. Sadly, later in his life he became addicted to Heroin. He went on to introduce me to my first experience of a Magic Mushroom Festival. This was held in Dibbinsdale Woods. That was before they bulldozed the area and built a dirty great big housing estate on this wonderful land. At the time of our festival the land was alive with endless wooded areas, streams, fields and wild life. It was perfect for a Magic Mushroom Festival. A camp was set up with a huge tepee, a fire, plus loads of teenagers. I had invited my best friend Vrony. Everyone there was on some sort of drug. We had taken Magic Mushrooms. I was crying with laughter, tears rolling down my face when I turned round to look at someone who I swear was the Queen. Outside people were sliding down hills, landing in the streams as the rain poured. Again I was in hysterics as to me they looked like the Ready Brek advert with the red golden glow around them. I don't know how long we were there as the element of time had been completely lost. Sadly. Some of the people went on a bad journey known as downers. This had an effect on the us all and the party fizzled out. We all dispersed going our separate ways. It was an adventure I shall never forget. Luckily for me I never became addicted to drugs.

When I eventually return home I am expecting no one to be in but as I approach the house I see lights on. I glance through the front window to see who is home. I am flabbergasted. I see my brother with his girlfriend. At first its hard for me to make out but as my eyes adjust to the scene. I see my brother's girlfriend on her knees. What on earth is she doing on her knees I think to myself. To my horror I realise what I am witnessing. He has his willy out and she is giving him a blow job.......

My friend Vrony and I are now dabbling in a bit of alcohol. Its usually Pomagne as that's the cheapest plonk that we can afford. We would sit in the cemetery drinking it through a straw. Apparently drinking alcohol through a straw enables you to get drunker quicker. We spend some evenings sitting in shop door ways with the local boys as we try to get passer's by to go into the off licence for us. At the weekends we would get the bus down town to Birkenhead Market. We spent our time wandering round the shops, dressed up to the nines to gain interest from boys. On one day at the market we even stole a lip gloss as a dare. We didn't have much money to do much else but we had fun, memorable times during this incredible, enlightening year of 1979.

We are in our last year of school. The big wide world of the unknown is ahead of us. Final school exams are looming. It is time to knuckle down to some serious revision. It is also time to start thinking seriously about what you intend to do when you leave school. We had it drummed into us how to address a letter, compose a letter and address an envelope for future job applications. I didn't learn very much from school to be fair. I can remember how to type. The vowels A E I O U. I learnt that detention wasn't a good place to be. I learnt everything about the Egyptians. I knew everything about Great Expectations. The book that is! I found out I couldn't sing! All I did know is that I was good at English and Art. Lastly I learnt how to dissect a bull's eye. Apart from this I didn't learn very much from my five years of attending this school. I can compose a great letter though!

It's the beginning of 1980 I am readying myself to take my final exams. At this crucial time, I have to go into hospital for quite a serious operation. My mum has accepted an out patient appointment for me to go in hospital to have a procedure done. I am excited but also very scared. The only time I had been in hospital was to have my tonsils and adenoids out at the once lovely Clatterbridge Hospital, which is a shadow of its former self. This time I am going into Arrow Park to have my big ears pinned back so that I don't have Dumbo ears anymore. The timing wasn't ideal really it would eventually have a detrimental effect on my exam results.

I go into hospital under the care of the wonderful Mr Drummond a ENT specialist. The procedure entails a needle being inserted into the ear cartilage so that they can hold the ear into its new position. Once this is done they can fix the cartilage to the bone behind the ear. This is done under general anaesthetic, generally taking two hours. I can't remember the operation. I can remember the pain. My head is wrapped like a mummy with bandages. I have to stay at home for two weeks. I scratched my head to bits desperate to wash my hair.

Finally, the dressings come off, I have new ears. I am over the moon. My ears are still sore and various shades of blue and purple. I am allowed to go back to school as long as I don't get my ears knocked. Two weeks doesn't sound like a lot of time to be off school but I had missed so much. I had missed vital tutorials and help with revision. Then some plonker hit me in my ear with a football which really hurt and set me back further. Hence I didn't do very well in my exams and my results were not great.

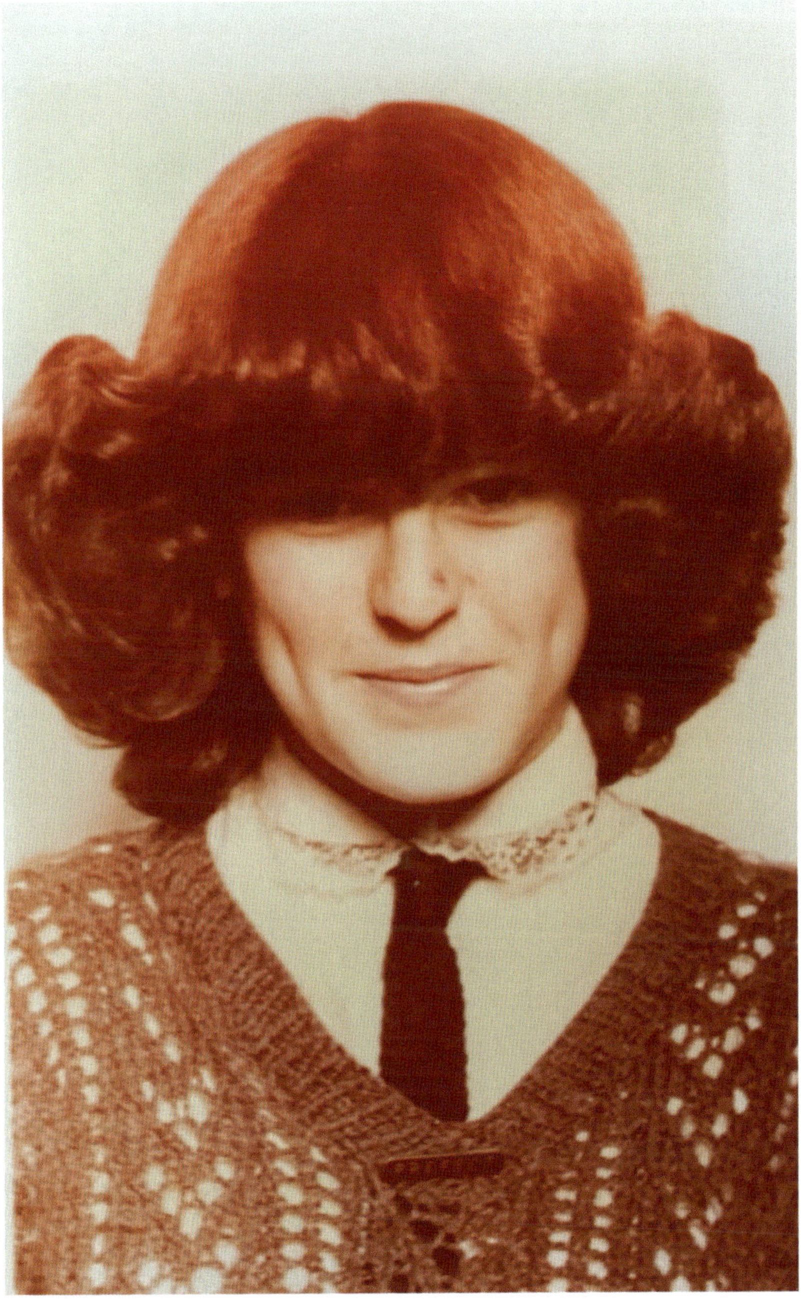

We all have our final class photo taken called the class of 79 although its now 1980. We are all wearing shitty brown, let me explain. In your final year at school in the 5th form we are allowed to stand out by having a different coloured uniform from the rest of the school. We all have to vote what colour we would like. Brown won the most votes so brown wins and we all walk round looking like little turds. Its final reports, the last year disco. It's the time to say goodbye to your favourite teachers and friends while putting the V up to the ones you wanted to forget, but will always remember. Its time to go off to the dole office to sign on to receive your Giro Cheque. Once I left school I never did see anyone from my school years. We all went our separate ways. I tell a lie I did have fleeting moments of HI in a pub once in a while. Now this is the question we ask ourselves. What do we want to be when we grow up? At one point I wanted to be a Nun, safe and protected from this scary world. Then I wanted to be a Stripper, the very opposite side of the coin. I finally decide that I want to be a check out girl at the local CO-OP. My mum has other ideas.

My mum tells me that I have to go to college, that I need to make something of myself.

I search for all the courses available at the local college. The college is not far from where I live its call Carlett

Park College. Carlett Park was an educational institution that goes back to the 1940s. It was once one of the top six colleges that trained people to the level of graduation. In the 70s it specialised in engineering science. A number of students came over to study from overseas as far as Iran. The wonderful Paul O'Grady studied there. Have a guess what it is now????? Yes. It's a huge housing estate as the college was ploughed down. The only remaining piece of its original history that is left is the family chapel that dates back to 1884.

Don't ask me why, as even I don't know why to this day but I opted to do the Hairdressing Course. This was a two year course which included Beauty Therapy, Communications, Business Organisations, Art, Wig Making and oddly Cookery. As my mum didn't have much money coming in I was able to get a small grant to pay for all the equipment I would need for this course. When all the equipment arrived at our house I marvelled at it with wonder and dismay. In September of 1980 at just 16, I started my college course with a lot of trepidation. The college was about a half hour walk from my home. After crossing the busy New Chester Road. I would walk down the never ending drive that led to the main entrance. The college was huge, vast, a maze of corridors. I regularly got lost for the first few months. My class was all female. They were all very nice girls. I found my course extremely difficult as I was left handed, so when I was looking and learning it was all the opposite way round. I found my practical lessons very challenging. At lunch times we would sit and chat in the huge student canteen. I had never seen so many young people in one place. We would be surrounded by members of the opposite sex, loitering with intent and ogling at the new meat. I didn't have much interest in boys until I set eyes on a beautiful young man of 20, I will stick with boy! He just oozed kerb appeal for me and shined through all the other boys there. I batted my eyelashes, blushing. Pretending not to stare. I hadn't had much experience with boys but when I saw him it was the first time I had felt tummy flutters. I would gaze longingly across the canteen. We would smile at each other saying nothing only speaking with our eyes. One day he spoke to me, I almost curled up and died. I blushed crimson.

Meanwhile I had carried on going to the night club Leighton Court. One night at the night club there he stood. I couldn't believe my eyes. He asked me to dance. At that moment all my dreams came true. He had dreamy eyes a floppy fringe and a gorgeous smile. He wore tight tight jeans with boots OMG and he smelt divine. We danced to Don't stand so close to me. That night I left the night club with my friend walking on air.

We didn't have mobile phones then so I had to wait until Monday at college to see him again. Oh dear I was smitten. He was finishing an apprenticeship in engineering which was held on the ground floor. As I came to college each morning I would have to pass his classroom and we would wave to each other. I was in love from the word go. I would only have to look at him and I would die and go to heaven in a heart beat. He was four years older than me but that didn't bother us. I felt so grown up, I finally had a proper boyfriend.

Meanwhile back to reality, I am still very conscious of my green teeth. I am sixteen and my jaw apparently is fully grown. I can now begin the long haul of many dental appointments. I cannot express the pain I had to endure to require new teeth. The procedure consists of filing my original teeth down until they resemble a fang. I wish they had knocked me out for this. They then attach temporary teeth until they have made your new ones. The whole thing is drawn out and extremely painful. The torture continued for six months until finally I have my permanent crowns fitted that are cemented to my original teeth. When I reach home I run to the hall mirror. I have lived my life with green stumpy teeth, I have not smiled in public, I have been teased for my ugly teeth. As I look at my reflection in the mirror, I laugh, I cried in dismay as I looked at my new teeth. I looked like Bugs Bunny. It was going to take a long time to get used to these bad boys as they were much larger than the teeth I had before. This was not the end of the teeth saga I can tell you. In future years I was to endure abscesses, tooth loss and always carried round with me a tube of super glue. Anyway I can now smile, I have flat ears and I have a boyfriend. Life is kinda good.

I am sixteen and a half to be precise. My time has come. I am on the point of losing my virginity. This is a massive thing for me. I am nervous. I am anxious. I have every feeling that can possibly course through a young woman who is about to give up her virginity. I have high expectations on how this is going to happen. I am thinking of when where and so on as I know that this is the scenario for me as I have had a boyfriend for a while so its bound to happen. I want this special moment to be romantic, gradual and above all I want it to be a magical moment that I will remember and recall as being the best way to lose your virginity. This is a once in life time experience. It should be a special time of sharing your body with someone important, someone that you truly love and who you know loves you the same.

I am home alone watching Donna Summer in concert. I am wearing my thick winceyette nightie with a pattern of tiny roses on it. I have it buttoned right up to my neck. No thoughts invaded me, I am innocently just watching Donna Summer on no particular night. My boyfriend turns up at the house in his shiny red Capri. He knocks at the door. I let him in. I am surprised to see him. We sit watching the Donna Summer concert. He lifts up my nightie with his warm soft hand. I am aware that I am naked underneath. There is no eye contact, no kisses, no caresses. There are no meaningful words said. I am not sure what to expect. He pulls my legs gently apart. Suddenly I feel penetration. He is riding me up and down a bit like a horse. I feel nothing. It does not excite me. Nor do I feel any sensation. I lay back thinking of England. I am still watching the concert over his head. I hear a sigh. I feel wetness between my legs. Its done. All my dreams are shattered in an instant. He sits up. He speaks words to me that shock me. "You didn't bleed." "That means you were not a virgin." I am stuttering as I reply. "I have never had sex with anyone this is my first time." He kneels before me. "Usually a woman bleeds when its her first time." I am totally bewildered. There is no compassion in his eyes as he said these words. I am numbed into silence. This was to be my first giant mistake.

That night I went to bed bewildered, confused and wondering what on earth had just occurred. Tears of sadness spilled over. I fell into a fitful sleep with an overwhelming feeling of I wish I had never done this.

Dear Cathy and Claire from Jackie did not prep me up for this. I should surely be waking up the next day feeling amazing. I felt shit when I woke up. I had to go to college and face the music. Nothing untoward happened really to be honest. I felt let down but he said nothing and we continued to see each other. Not that he took me anywhere. We ended up being like rabbits at it anywhere, any time any place. As I look back on this whole experience, he never seemed to be interested in whether I was enjoying the sex or even being satisfied. He had me giving him blow jobs and sex in random places. He never once asked if I was alright or if I was enjoying it. Sadly. I was smitten I was prepared to do exactly what he wanted me to do even if it meant that I was left dissatisfied. I just wanted to keep him happy. We were in love weren't we? This is what I was supposed to do. I was content in the thought that I was doing everything I should be doing. I was in the mind set that this is how it should be. He appeared to be happy.

It was only when I reached my late 50s that I realised after the sexual encounters I had experienced over my life time that there is a difference in having sex and making love. I can tell you that there is an immense difference. It is probably the most amazing experience that you will ever encounter to be made love to.

Then I was naïve, green as the grass, young stupid, uneducated in this area. I have let many men gratify themselves without giving any thought for me. Never again!!!!

I stay with my boyfriend Mike. I am giving him hand jobs whilst watching Brookside with his mum and dad in their lounge. Crazy I know. I was intent on keeping him happy whatever it took. I put all my feelings aside until one day it all backfired.

Some advice ladies. Never let a man take advantage of you. If he doesn't put you first, respect you or have your back and doesn't support you in your times of need or look after you when you are sick. Then he is not good enough for you. You are worth so much more.

Now 1981 I am almost seventeen. Mike and I had never discussed contraception. I had never discussed this with anyone. I hadn't even thought about it. I also didn't have anyone I could confide in about this topic.

The day came. A dark thunderous cloud descended on to us. I have missed a period. I miss another and still the penny did not drop. Eventually after a few months I decide to take myself off to the local clinic. I was given a pregnancy test. I had discussions with the kindly nurse which much embarrassment on my part to decide what options I had and which contraception's where available to me. I was given a box of condoms and a prescription for birth control. All a bit to late really as I am given the news that I am pregnant. I catch the bus to Mike's house to give him the news. I am unprepared for his reaction. He wasn't happy. He carefully explained to me what we had to do. What had to be done. I felt so sad and lonely as I travelled back home on the next bus. My world had fallen apart.

I couldn't tell my Mum. She was now busy with her new husband and extended family. She seems so happy in her new life. Her new husband Roy Boy has moved into our family home. I now have a Step Dad. My brothers have all left home. My mum would go nuts if I tell her so I decide to tell no one. Mike and I manage to keep this dark secret under wraps.

My boyfriend Mike kindly organises for me to go to an abortion clinic in Liverpool. A date is arranged for me to go to a day centre/hospital somewhere in Liverpool to have my pregnancy terminated. That is the day I shall never forget. It's my 17th Birthday. I am spending it lying on an operating table. I cannot remember everything. I am a believer that our minds have a clever way of switching off to painful memories that are too hard to recall. I can only explain in my own words that there was a machine a bit like a hoover that sucks the foetus out of you. I feel numb to what is taking place and to what is actually happening to me. I am sent to a large canteen which is packed with young girls, young women. They are sobbing, sniffing, pan faced and some in shear shock. It was all extremely disturbing. I don't know how I got to the train station. I can remember Mike meeting me. He is holding a giant Teddy Bear. He smiles as he says "Happy Birthday." We board the train. He escorts me home where I am greeted with presents and cards for my 17th Birthday. I pushed my emotions aside into a place within my heart. I smiled. I said thank you. I put on a front. I pretended all was okay and that nothing had ever happened. A few days later as I am practicing my new found hairdressing skills on one of my step dad's family member a situation occurs. We are all in the front room. I am cutting her fringe when I am overcome with extreme pain in my stomach. My mum is shouting to me. "What's wrong Karen." Her face is distorted with fear. As we look, we all witness blood flowing down my legs. There are pieces of what I can only describe as red chunks of bloody flesh. I am not sure what happened next. I find myself on a table in surgical surroundings. I feel like I am having an abortion all over again. Later it is explained to me that some of the after birth had been left inside of me. I am assured that they have managed to remove it all now. I don't know how I got home. The whole incident was never discussed. The whole affair was swept under the carpet by everyone including me. It was never ever talked about. Life goes back to normal. I return to college after a short break. I carry on with my studies. I carry on seeing my boyfriend.

At college the yearly hairdressing competitions begin. As I have the longest hair in class I am asked to be a model this becomes a regular occurrence until I have virtually no hair left. I have always regretted having my hair cut short and I was convinced that this had an impact on my relationship with Mike. It was when he first saw me with short hair which was a few weeks after the dreaded abortion took place that he decides to split up with me. I am chucked. I am dumped without an explanation. I am completely heart broken that he could do this to me at such a bad time. Is there a good time to finish a relationship with someone? Maybe not!!!!!

This was the moment that my mental health issues start to rear their ugly head.

So much of my past had been buried. Problems went unsupported. Issues were never discussed.

This scenario opened up all my wounds that had not healed properly.

The very next day I woke up with a feeling of despair. I had a plan…. I got up early, leaving for college earlier than I normally would. In my bag I had packed all that I needed to carry out my plan. I had a bottle of water, razor blades and a bottle of pills. At the college there is a basement were there are female toilets. No one really used them. They were out of the way so I knew I wouldn't be disturbed. I locked myself in one of the toilets and began to slice my wrists with a razor blade, trying desperately to hit a vein. I swallow as many tablets as I can manage to get down my throat. I am sobbing as I watch the blood dripping onto the floor. The blood splattered up the door and onto the cold tiles. I am not aware of how long I was there. Its so quiet there, I am feeling tired I am feeling faint. I stand, I clutch the handle. I feel unsteady on my feet. I feel disorientated. I stagger out of the toilets, up the stairs and down the long lane to head to a bus stop. I wasn't sure where I was going. Everything is a bit hazy. The next thing I know I am in Deva.

Deva was opened in 1829. It was known as The Cheshire Lunatic Asylum. In 1921 it changed its name to County Mental Hospital. In 1941 it was called Upton Mental Hospital. In 1950 it was renamed Deva Hospital. In 1983 it was known as The Countess of Chester. The Asylum closed in 1991. It was demolished in 2008 and guess what? Yes, it became a housing estate.

My wrists are bound tightly with bandages. I am wheeled down to another room to have my stomach pumped. Nothing is said to me by anyone. I finally lay in bed feeling sleepy when all of a sudden my youngest brother appears. He is asking me "Why." I am not given any support. I am not offered any therapy. I am discharged and sent home. I am not sure how I got home from Chester to Bromborough.

Once again nothing is said. The whole incident is never talked about. The whole event went under the carpet along with the rest of the shit!!!!

I return to college. I return to life in general as if nothing has ever happened.

I feel so stupid now that I begged Mike to get back with me like some desperate fool, allowing myself like an idiot, a love sick puppy to this man. I tried everything to keep him or else I felt as if I had nothing to live for. To the point that I made a complete hash of my life all in the name of what I thought was love….

It is now 1982 I am nearing the age of eighteen. I am nearing the end of this journey.

It is a well known fact that war, violence, sexual abuse, verbal abuse, emotional abuse, mental abuse, domestic abuse and bullying for the young and old leads to a life long psychological consequences that manifests into educational difficulties, low self esteem, depression causing trouble in forming and maintaining relationships.   Children exposed to this as adults are more likely to abuse drugs and alcohol, suffer from depression, anxiety and post traumatic disorders. It can cause nightmares. Those children who have experienced abuse can have trouble paying attention in school and find it harder to cope with life stresses that can in turn cause mental health problems. They can go on to find it difficult to be a parent. They can show signs of harmful behaviour to themselves. They may find it difficult to make and keep friends. They may become withdrawn, have problems with identifying feelings or communicating their needs. This in turn can create struggles with separation and more.

It is the 1980s. Its now 2024. So why the FUCK are we still doing all of this abuse to each other??????????? Haven't we learnt anything?????? It is unbelievable that in this day and age that this still goes on. That it is allowed to go on. We as a human race have learnt nothing. It is far easier to love, support, respect and be kind to others and the ones we love than to cause unnecessary pain and long term suffering.

1982 was an eventful year. The Falkland war is happening, Ozzy Osbourne decides to to shock us all by eating a bat live on stage and a new Prince is being born.

I am almost eighteen and nearing the end of my hairdressing college course. I am still in a relationship with Mike. I try as often as I can to see him. I would get the bus to Garden City and walk to the garage where he frequently went to do work on his precious Capri. I would sit in the office, make him cups of tea while living in the hope that he would stop what he was doing to be with me. He rarely did. I stoop so low as to pay for his petrol so he would come and see me. I would allow him to have sex with me, fooling myself that he loved me.

I laugh when I look back and remember the time when we were having full blown sex on my single bed. My mum barged in shouting. "Karen have you ate all the yoghurts?" I called back over Mike's shoulder. "No Mum." She never batted an eyelash. She just tutted, shut the door and went.

How low can you go???? I went lower. I would get the bus to his house, blow dry his hair for him to go on a date with his ex girlfriend who he had a child to. I am ashamed of myself for the lengths I went to just to see him. I lost all self respect for myself. I lost who I was through my obsession for this person. I was craving love. I wanted to feel needed and wanted to obtain everything I wasn't getting at home.

The worst was yet to come…….

At almost eighteen I foolishly make a huge boo boo. I stop taking my contraception as I am not really seeing Mike any more. After a sexual encounter with him I become pregnant.

Will he come back to me? I tell him the news. His reaction is. "I will never marry you." Although he did buy me an engagement ring!!!!!

I childishly leave a letter for me mum as I didn't have the nerve to tell her face to face. I also tell her that I have run away and I actually tell her where I have run away to.

I fool myself into believing that Mike will stay with me this time. I day dream of our future together with our baby, living in a little house happily ever after.

This was a dream that was never realistically going to happen as my mum steps in with a plan for us to sort this situation out. We go along with her plans.

It is 1982 which doesn't seem that long ago. Peoples views, their outlook on things were still very old fashioned. People having babies out of wed lock was still frowned upon. There were still young women getting sent away secretly to mother and baby homes.

I was about to be one of those young women. My mum begins to tell family and friends that I have gone off to work in Jersey. Mean while I am ordered to stay out of sight. I am not allowed to go out of the house. If any visitors come to the house I was locked in the pantry. Many times I was sent to the pantry to sit in the dark for hours or sent to my bedroom to sit against the bedroom door until the visitors had gone. These situations proved to be detrimental for me in my future life as I have a fear of small spaces, closed doors and over crowded areas. During this time I just thought that my mum was trying to protect me by doing what she did. That it was all for my own good. As time passed buy it became harder and harder to keep me hidden. Family and friends began to start asking questions.

My mum made the decision to contact the Salvation Army. They directed her to obtain the help from the church. I was sent to a safe house in Altrincham to live with a family of religious background. I moved in with this family into their large Victorian home. I had my own room. I was to help around the house, be polite and do what I was told. I begin to literally start pulling strands of my hair out. I would be told off by the nuns for making a mess on the floor. I didn't go out, I had no visitors or phone calls. I was sad and lonely with a feeling of abandonment. I don't know how long I lived with this family but I knew it was long enough for me to scream to leave.

While I was there I wrote a couple of letters to Mike. He did write back telling me all about his holiday in Spain. He even enclosed a photograph of him and his mates with a girl in a skimpy bikini in his arms. I cried of course. I immediately wrote to my mum telling her if she didn't come and get me and take me home that I would run away. I hated living with this strange family and I loathed my visits with the Nuns.

I was taken back to my home in Bromborough by my mum and my step dad. I was relieved to be home. Little did I know how short this stay was going to be. I was desperate to see Mike. I secretly left the house and caught the bus to Deeside. I turned up unexpectedly at his parent's house. Mike wasn't best pleased to see me. He escorted me back to the bus stop saying that I wasn't allowed to be there. We argued. I stormed off and began my long walk from Deeside to Bromborough. Halfway home I could see Mike's car pull up beside me as he shouted at me to get into the car. I told him to get stuffed! I don't know how I managed it, maybe from pent up emotions, anger, determination or stupidity but I walked the eleven miles which took me over four hours to get to Bromborough. It was now dark as I headed to the chippy as I was starving. Frantically I dipped into my hot tasty chips. As I looked up I saw my brother driving past in his work's van. He looked straight at me. I hid in the bushes until he was out of sight. Shit! I am going to be in big trouble now. I told my mum about the incident. Sadly, this led to me being sent away yet again into hiding. My bags were packed. I am taken by the Nuns to a Nunnery. The place is called St Bridget's, number 15 Lache Lane, Chester. It's a large Victorian building set in beautiful grounds that is run by the Nuns. I am met at the main entrance by a happy smiling Nun who took me under her wing. St Bridget's mother and baby home opened its doors in 1949, it took in many young women who were in need of accommodation and support due to their unfortunate circumstances. Today it is no longer there as it is now a housing estate. I enter the large entrance hall. I am then shown to my room. My room is very basic but comfy. I have everything I need and the window looked out onto the grounds. I also have a secret door that leads into the bathroom. I can go through this door and lock the other entrance from the landing so it feels like I have an en-suite. This was all very good until eventually I grew too big to fit through the secret doorway. The rest of the nunnery was vast and consisted of a large communal dining area. A laundry room for us all to do our washing. There was a conservatory that is used as a place to meet up with friends and family who visit. There is a separate part of the nunnery that is lived in by young Mums who have had their baby and receive support for helping them to look after their child. This is where I meet my first friend Janice. Janice is 19 she has a young baby called Nathan. She is from Liverpool. She doesn't have any teeth! Janice is very friendly and welcoming. When I ask her why she is here she explains that she wasn't able to look after her baby properly. Janice is often visited by a young man of a similar age. They meet regularly in the conservatory which is for visitors. Each time he visits it is to have sex with her. She laughs about this as she tells me. I am in shock as to what is going on especially as the conservatory is all glass windows. Turns out the fella is Nathans dad!!!!

There is another girl called Donna. She is a young girl living there with her baby as she has no where to go. She has no money or family to help her.

In the other quarters lives a girl called Janet who is heavily pregnant who is planning to have her baby adopted. She explains she can't wait for it to be all over so she can get back to normal.

Another girl called Elaine from Stockport is the youngest girl there. Elaine is totally undecided as to whether to keep her baby or not. Then there is me. I am told that I am having my baby adopted. The process for adoption is already in process. We are all in similar situations. I am sure if we were older with the right support, money, life skills then we wouldn't be here. But we were. We laughed, we joked and generally just got on with things the best we could. We are all allowed £6 a week to spend. We are on a 9pm curfew. Every day was more or less the same. We all waited for a letter or a visit from friends and family. It was so exciting when one of us received a parcel or a letter from someone. Even if it came from the benefits office! Once a week we walked into Chester. We walked round window shopping dreaming of the things we would like to buy. At the home we were fed, watered, we had our own room and a comfy bed. We were all given jobs to do around the home. We were safe we had a roof over our head all paid for by the benefit system. We all attended the local Ante natal classes. We don't take them very seriously. They are telling us how we should breast feed our babies even though we are not keeping them. There are couples there who are all loved up excited about becoming a family. The classes were hard for us due to the fact although we were encouraged to go for health reasons for the baby it was a difficult situation to be in when you are not going to have your baby at the end of it all. My mum and step dad visited me once while I was living there. They stayed for about an hour. They gave me a few quid then left. Mike came to see me once. We talked, we laughed and joked about where I was living and talked about the mad scenarios at the home. He did take me out one day. He took me to the River Dee. He shagged me on the bench then took me back home. He says he has to go as he has to get to work. I was so happy to see him that I didn't have the sense to realise that he was using me. He has a job in a night club. I don't see him again while I am living at St Bridget's. He did write to me once.

MIKE STERRY
93 SANDY LANE
GARDEN CITY
SEALAND
DEESIDE.

Dear Edgeypoos
How are you diddling lad. I bet you thought I wouldn't write back didn't you? Well I thought you might smash me up if I didn't, so I did. I'm only messing Edgey, I said I would write you a letter and here is. How's life treating you at St Bridget. I would love to see your cleaner in person you know, that one in Studio 4½ under the title Bridget at work, the one that looks like you. (I'm only messing lub, you know I lub you as you are, even if you've got a 6 inch belly button).
Anyway I'll have to go now to wash my car.

From
Mike.

I am now 7 months pregnant. Things are about to change. Before I was pregnant I was of a slim build. I was 8 and a half stone, 5ft 6, I was curvy. Mike used to say I reminded him of a page 3 model. I was over the moon when he said this to me as it meant so much to have a compliment. This was the nicest compliment that he ever paid me apart from I gave good head!!!!!!!!! I am now 16 stone

I can't wear normal shoes as my feet won't fit in them so I have to wear slippers all the time. I have to wear large smock dresses. My legs and ankles hurt so much. When I have a bath my body feels like its on fire, its so painful. My hands are swollen, my face is big and round. My breasts are humongous and hurt like hell. I am doing everything to stay healthy. I don't drink, I rarely smoke. I am taking all my supplements as instructed. I haven't a clue why I am so large. I attend all my usual check ups at the hospital. They do the usual blood pressure check, blood tests, pelvic examination, ultra sounds and urine tests. Today when I go for my check up their faces are showing signs of concern. They tell me everything is okay. I return to my home. I start to miss my Ante natal classes. I am not bothered about how to breast feed my baby and how it will benefit my child or how safe it is. How it contains anti bodies which help to protect your baby. I feel out of place when I go there as I will never be able to do this. My baby is up for adoption. Mike and I have filled in all the relevant paper work. We have talked about matching up eye colour, hair and skin colour. We have discussed family backgrounds. We have gone through all the history of illness, defects and genetics. It is all very difficult for us both. We are this babies parents. We are preparing to give our child away. We are both young, too young to realise the severity of the situation.

We didn't think about how this was going to affect our families or us. I wasn't even sure whether I could go through with it all. There are so many voices in my head. So much advice given by my mum, by the nuns and by Social Services. Mike never really said much.

Sadly. The whole tidal wave of emotions is taken out of my hands…. Christmas passes in a blur. I am almost 8 months pregnant. I can't think about the Falklands war or about ET being a major film. I can't think about Michael Jackson's release of Thriller. My body is in agony. My baby is kicking. I can feel its little toes pressing against me. I can feel it doing somersaults. I feel its life. I touch my stomach the movements amaze me. We created this tiny human being. I imagine how it will look and what colour hair it will have. I think about how this baby will need someone to love it, protect it, keep it safe from harm, provide for it. It will need someone to give it the life that it deserves. Give it a world full of love, care and attention.

What can I give it? I can love it but I have nothing else to offer. I have no home, no money, no stability and no support. What can I give an innocent child that I am about to bring into this world.

I cry in the night for answers to my personal questions.

At 8 months pregnant I am rushed into hospital. My urine sample is showing Protein +++. I don't know what this means. I am put on to a ward and I have a bed next to a lovely woman, who is also called Karen. She is about to give birth to her first child. She is so excited. We are both ordered to stay on bed rest. I find this really difficult. I can't just lie in bed and do nothing. The nurses are constantly checking up on me, taking urine samples, blood samples and my blood pressure. I behave like a naughty school girl as I always go missing taking myself off to the smoke room. How mad does that sound when then a pregnant woman could go and have a cigarette and that they actually had a room for you!!! Billows of smoke filled the room to be fair you didn't need to smoke as there was enough smoke in there to inhale without having to smoke. If I wasn't in the smoke room I was in the toilet or roaming the corridors talking to people. I am constantly being told off for my behaviour.

All of a sudden I am being transferred to the Labour suite. I am surrounded by all kinds of surgical apparatus and nursing staff. I am told I have Pre-eclampsia toxaemia and oedema

Pre-eclampsia toxaemia causes foetus growth restriction it affects the arteries that carry blood to the placenta. If left untreated it can lead to a coma. It can be fatal to both the mother and the baby. It can cause damage to the kidneys, lungs, heart and eyes. It can cause a stroke or brain injury. It can cause high blood pressure. The oedema is brought on by severe pre-eclampsia. It can happen with your first pregnancy. It shows up in the urine as protein. It is paramount to induce the labour. It can also cause low birth weight.

Through the glass window I can see my mum and step dad. The situation is serious. They are asked if anything happens who would you want to save as now I am on the verge of going into a coma. Time is of the essence. My mum is made to choose between me and my baby.

Everything is black and hazy after that. The next thing I know is I can hear a baby crying. Its my baby. It's a baby boy weighing in at 7lb. I am aware that someone is saying to me. "Have you a name for your baby?" I can't speak. My baby is rushed away. As they realise that this baby is up for adoption. I haven't been able to hold him, to feel his warmth, to smell his newness, to feel love for this beautiful baby. I watch confused as he is taken away.

Here I am left in a room on my own. After all the chaos I am left alone with my thoughts and feelings which are all over the shop. An Asian consultant in a white coat enters the room. He asks me if I am okay. He asks me how I am feeling. Before I have a chance to digest this information he is touching my breasts in a sexual manner. He asks me how they are feeling. Inside of me I am questioning if this is normal for someone to be doing this. After a bit he stops and leaves the room. It is 15/01/83. I have given birth to a gorgeous baby boy who has been taken away with a small band on his wrist bearing the name Michael Edge. I still have his wrist band. After some time I am transferred upstairs to a ward where there are all new mums with their babies by their side. I feel empty, alone and completely bereft in what has just happened. I hear the new born babies crying in the night. I hear the new mums cooing over their babies it is painful and unbearable. I have no one to talk to, I am left alone with my thoughts. I sleep fitfully after a long day of trauma. I am woken regularly to be checked upon.

As days passed while I am left to get better. I cannot stand it any longer. I plead and beg my mum and Mike to let me keep my baby. I ask to see my baby. I am taken down to a private room. My baby is lying peacefully in a hospital cot. There are no balloons, no cards of congratulations, no nothing. I look at his mop of dark hair. I look at his tiny feet and hands. I take in the feeling of helplessness for us both. I want to touch him feel him, hold him, give him my love. I want to give him the reassurance that I will be there for him no matter what. I don't want to let go of my tiny baby. I give him the name Matthew Jan. I make the huge decision to keep my boy. Because I am still recovering I am made to stay in the hospital for two weeks. I am taught how to feed my baby. I am shown how to bathe my son. I am shown how to change his nappy and how to wind him. I am taught by the staff how I should care for my son.

Once again a decision made by others occurs and the whole thing is taken out of my hands as social services step in.

Matthew is taken into temporary foster care.

This is done for a reason. The reason being is that I am not well enough to look after him. I return to my family home without my son. I say goodbye to the old me, Karen, I say goodbye to St Bridget's. I never did see or hear from anyone from there again.

Matthew is taken to live with a foster family not far away while I recover. He goes to live in temporarily foster care in Bromborough Pool. The plan is that I am to go over to the foster parents in time for feeds, bathing and bed time. I tried so hard. Every time I went over they had already done what I was supposed to be doing. This went on for some weeks until I said that something wasn't right. Eventually social services intervened and I got to take him to my mum's house. I was so excited to bring him home. I lay him on the bed. I talked to him. I played with him, I cuddled him and began bonding with my son. My middle brother was there with his girlfriend. They helped me to change his nappy as he peed on my brother's girlfriend's face we all laughed. I felt content that I had my son. I don't have a pram to take him out. I don't have my mum's approval. I just have an overwhelming feeling that I want to love and provide for my son.

Things change and good news is on the horizon……

Mike brings the best news. He has managed to secure a house for us that we can rent. The house is in Garden City it has a garden for Matthew and its just round the corner from his mum and dad. I was over the moon. At last we could be together, we could now be a proper family. We didn't have much in the way of furnishings but we had what we needed. I was so looking forward to the move. I could have my son back full time. I dreamed of making house for us all. It was going to be wonderful.

This moment was short lived when Mike dropped a bomb shell, shattered my dreams as he announced that he had finally got a job. This would have been great but the job was in Butlins in Minehead as an engineer. He convinced me that it would not be for long. He assured me that he would send me money regularly, that he would visit us often. I moved in with my son to 18 Garden City Deeside. I was naturally feeling apprehensive. This was such a huge step in my life. I tried to remain positive and busy by making house. I painted Matthew's nursery with images of clowns and the alphabet creating a colourful happy room for him to sleep in. I made the lounge as homely as I could. It was so hard for me as I didn't have a washing machine so I would hand wash Matthew's nappies. I didn't have a cooker to cook on but to be fair I didn't really have any money for food. I relied on freebies from the local clinic to feed Matthew and I lived off Mars Bars. I rarely saw family or friends. Gradually I began to lose weight. I was starting to struggle to look after the house and a new baby. I would write to Mike and he would write back. He did visit once in the 6 months that he was away. In total he sent me £15 to help me out. I knew I was now seriously struggling alone. I was in dire straights. I applied for help for benefits which got rejected as I was now with Mike and as he was working, he was the one who should provide for us. As months passed by. I was desperate, I was lonely. I made one last ditch attempt to fight to get Mike to come home.

I do what I think is right at this time. I ask my mum to loan me enough money to buy a train ticket to Minehead. There are no mobile phones then and I didn't have a house phone either so I couldn't ring him to let him know. I asked his sister in law to look after Matthew for a couple of nights. I make the long journey to Minehead. When I arrive I find out that the camp is way out of town. I walk the long walk to Butlins holiday camp. I am thinking that Mike will be so pleased to see me. I arrive at the security gates and ask the guard if I can speak to Mike Sterry. I can see Mike walking towards me. He looks surprised and worried. I am so excited to see him. We walk and talk. I explain to him that I am struggling to manage. That Matthew and I are finding it difficult to live on the money he has sent. He takes me to the B&B that I am staying at. He didn't take me out, he didn't feed me. He has sex with me and tells me he can't come back that I should go back home to Matthew. I return to 18 Garden City feeling more alone than ever. I am at a loss as what to do next. I receive 3 letters in total from Mike and the sum of £15 for the three months that I live in Garden City. I am now down to 7 stone due to lack of food. I am feeling helpless and alone.

Thank you for making me

M. J. STERRY

STAFF NO 66636X

MAIN CATERING

BUTLINS HOLIDAY CENTRE

MINEHEAD

SOMERSET.

11/4/83.

Dear Edgeypoos

How are you feeling now love. I hope you are okay love. I know it must be hard for you to cope on your own with Matty and the house. I am really missing you and Matty so when are you going to send me some pictures of you both.

 but you know I have to work here for the Kissing is / please stick it out love because I don't want to lose either of you.

4/5/83

①

M J STERRY.

STAFF NO 66636X

MAIN CATERING

BUTLINS HOLIDAY CAMP

MINEHEAD

SOMERSET.

Dear Karen and Matty.

Thanks for your letters, especially the last one! Ever since I read the letter I have been thinking about your "best sin". I'm glad to hear you are coping alright lub.

come home for the weekend. I've still got this cold and cough. I can't seem to get rid of it. I'll h to buy some buttercup syrup or something like that. I've chan my working hours now. I have t do a shift in the morning and a shift at tea time. Some of the top managers came in to the kitchen and one of them asked me to hav a look at his car. I had a look it and fixed it for him. He wa made up so if I don't get a good reference from here I'll wan to know why. Anyway enough about work. I hope you and fa in the coal shed and you aren

1/6/83

MIKE STERRY
BUTLINS.

Dear Karen and Matty

How are you both keeping. I really enjoyed it when I came home It was great to see you and matty again
I have got the pictures developed and they are great. There are some really good ones of matty and some really good ones of you, if you know what I mean. I hope you and Matty have a nice time in Jersey you deserve a holiday so make the most of it and take it easy. I enclose a cheque for $15 for you. Anyway I'll get

Things are about to change. I am soon to be 19 and Mike is coming home.

It is 1983, it is July its my 19th Birthday. Mike has a lovely surprise for me. He returns home from Minehead. We are so excited to see him. We make love, I am so happy to have him home. The next day as we are sitting in the kitchen he looks at me. The radio is playing in the background. Love don't live here anymore by Rolls Royce. He makes an announcement. "We are over." To say that I was in shock is an understatement. I plead, I beg him but to no avail. "You will have to find somewhere else to live." "You can't stay here."

My whole world dropped out of my arse.

Social Services are brought in. They explain to Mike that legally he is allowed to make me leave but if he does then I will have no where to go and nor will Matthew. They ask him to reconsider. My social worker tries to make him realise that what he is doing is putting me in an awful situation. Mike doesn't change his mind. I am forced to leave. I wanted to scream, shout, cry, beg, plead for him to change his mind. I want to curl up and die. Mike looked at me with no emotion. "I am not going to change my mind."

Not one person, not my dad, not my mum, not my nan, not one of my three brothers, not my step dad, not one of Mike's family stepped in to give me support, love or help. No one came to my rescue to help me with what I was going through and what I was about to go through.

I sit here as I write and I can still feel the despair and pain I felt inside of me at this time. The pain of the predicament I was placed in both mentally and emotionally. Not one person came forward.

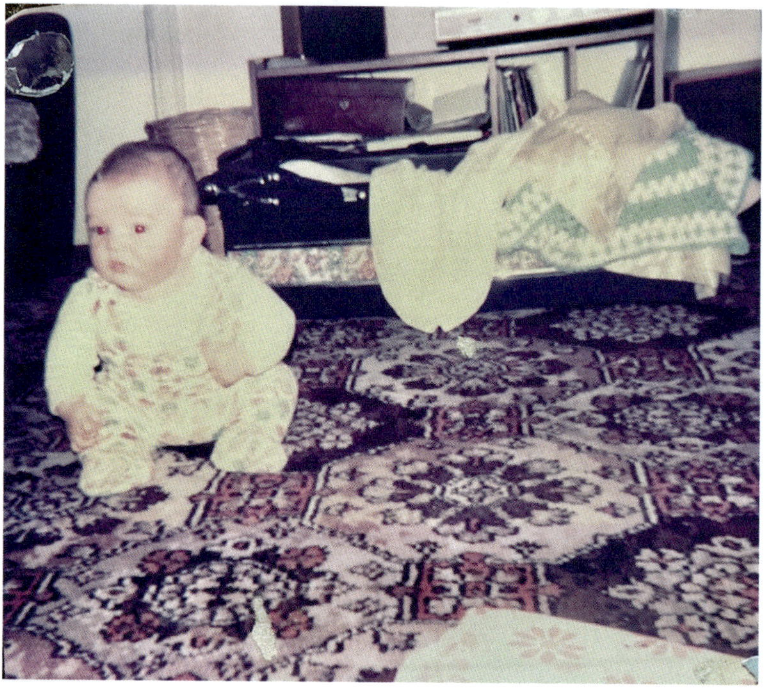

Luckily I had a lovely Social Worker. His name was Mr Lemon. I can still see him now. He was tall and thin he wore glasses and he was very quietly spoken. He looked at me sadly. I didn't want charity. I didn't want someone to feel sorry for me I wanted serious help. He excelled in trying to find a home for Matthew and I to go to. He did come up with a few options for me. He showed me a few bed-sits and rooms, which were hovels, in areas where you wouldn't want to keep even a dog. He apologised at what alternatives he was offering me. I was shitting myself for what the future had in store for us.

On the 27th of July 1983 I was ordered to leave 18 Garden City. The decision was taken out of my hands as I really didn't have anywhere to go. My step dad refused to let me move back home with Matthew and my mum stood by his decision. I had no other choice but to place Matthew into temporary foster care that Mr Lemon had arranged. Matthew went to live with a young family in Connahs Quay. I moved back home to live with my mum and step dad in their flat in Hornby Road Bromborough. I moved back into to a situation that was difficult. Cracks were beginning to appear in their three years of being married. It was obvious that my step dad didn't want me there. As soon as I moved back they began to argue. I felt responsible for this.

The arguing spiralled out of control to the point that my mum began to sleep with me. She slept with a knife under her pillow. Once again a repeat of domestic violence came back to haunt us. This became evident as I witnessed my step dad attempting to strangle my mum after an argument. She retaliated by giving him a black eye. My step dad began to order us around. We were made to have separate areas in kitchen cupboards and the fridge. If I wanted to wash my hair, I had to pay 50p. I had to pay to use the phone. It all became unbearable. I was reliving abuse from the past.

I began to fall into the depths of depression. I was at a loss as to what to do.

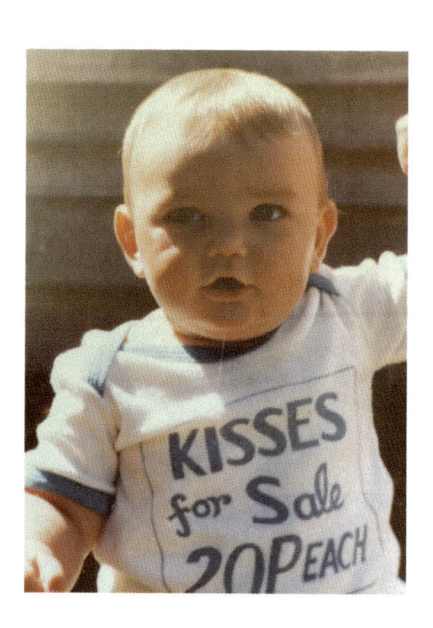

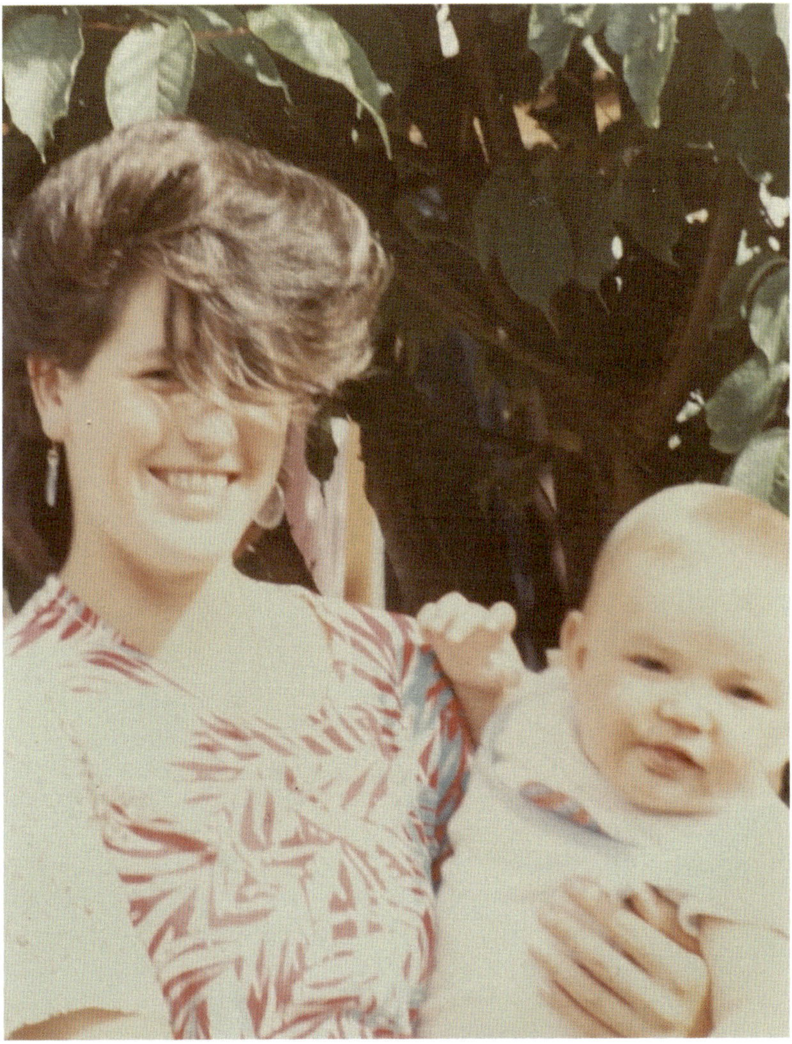

I would travel to Connahs Quay to visit Matthew as often as I could. I missed him so much. The home he was living at was beautiful. It had a huge garden. He had everything he could ask for. The family were also lovely and kind. Each time I left with a heavy heart. The couple's children would chase me down the road shouting at me not to come back. They would throw stones from their gravel drive at me. I watched as the foster parents appeared to be bonding with Matthew. One day I heard Matthew say "Da Da." To the foster dad. I felt deflated, my heart sank. Matthew seemed so happy, so well cared for, so loved. He was being given so much more than I would ever be able to give him. The crunch came when I made my usual visit. As I left I chucked my cigarette stump into the gutter. The children did their usual thing, chasing me down the street, throwing stones. The eldest son picked up the cigarette stump that was still alight and stubbed it into my back. I couldn't take it anymore. I had no one to explain to about what was going on here and at home. I wasn't coping, it was all proving to be too much for me. At the end of September 1983 I flipped.

Mike was now residing in 18 Garden City with his girlfriend whom he had been having a relationship with whilst he had been working in Butlins Minehead. He had moved her in as soon as I had left and they were going to be married. They planned to bring Matthew back to live with them. This was the straw that broke the camel's back.

I now had a new Social Worker. Her name was Sue Underwood. I asked her to visit me as I needed to talk to her. I vividly recall her sitting in my mum's flat. I tried to explain to her about what was going on at home. I tried to explain to her about the situation with the foster family. I tried to explain how I couldn't cope anymore that it was all getting me down. I sat crying as I made the ultimate decision that I was unable to provide for Matthew. I couldn't give him what he needed. I told her I would have to give him up. I will never ever, ever forget her response. She told me that I was making a bad decision. She remarked that how could I give up my child. She offered me no support. I was offered no alternative. I was offered no help as she looked at me with disgust.

How could she understand what I was going through or what I had already gone through. How could anyone? This was the biggest decision of my life. It wasn't what I wanted to do. It was Hobson's choice.

My whole world was falling apart at the seams.

My mum and step dad had started divorce proceedings.

Mike has taken me court to gain full custody of our son. I attend the Clwyd County Council Court in Mold. My Mum and friend Vrony are with me to provide moral support. Mike is sitting in the next room with his wife to be. It was a long winded and extremely painful court case.

I had made the decision to appeal to have Matthew adopted. Not because I didn't want him. Not because I didn't want Mike to have him. I did what I did for Matthew and for him alone. This was not easy for me. This decision destroyed me for the rest of my life.

Please do not judge me. Read the court papers and make your own decision. Try to understand my position. I did what I did at this time solely in the best interests of my son Matthew.

I walked away with nothing but a broken heart.

KAREN EDGE

ADVICE ON APPEAL

On 14th March 1984 I represented Miss Edge in her unsuccessful attempt to defend an application for custody under the Guardianship Of Minors Act 1971 by Michael John Sterry before the Mold Justices. The child Matthew Jan was born on 15th January 1983. On the birth of the child it was apparently decided by the parties that he should be adopted because there was no suitable accommodation in which they could keep him. In addition Miss Edge was physically unable to care for him owing to the fact that the birth had been a difficult one for her. As a result the child was placed in voluntary care on the 27th January 1983 but was returned to Miss Edge after a short time and she took him to live with her mother and step-father in Bromborough. At the beginning of April Miss Edge and the child moved into 18 Brookside City Deeside with Mr. Sterry where they intended to live as a family. However, a few days later Mr. Sterry obtained employment at a Butlins Holiday Camp in Minehead in Somerset and left Miss Edge and the child in Garden City.

The Department of Health and Social Security prevented Miss Edge from claiming Supplementary Benefit in her right and Mr. Sterry, with whom responsibility for her support now lay, sent her only a very small amount of money. There is a dispute between the parties as to the precise degree of financial support given by Mr. Sterry during his absence but on any view Miss Edge and the child were left in desperate financial straits during this time.

Mr. Sterry returned to Garden City at the end of June.

Their relationship steadily deteriorated until Mr. Sterry returned to Minehead on the 27th July and the relationship ended. On the same day the child Matthew was again placed into voluntary care whilst Miss Edge searched for suitable alternative accommodation. Mr. Sterry knew of this arrangement but neither he nor any member of either family were prepared to stop it and the child was given to foster parents where he presently remains. Initially Miss Edge exercised her rights to access but in the September of 1983 she reached the decision to leave Matthew with his foster parents as she felt unable to care for him and did not wish to disturb him any further. Her wish was that Matthew be adopted by a suitable couple and enjoy a normal, stable family relationship.

After leaving for Minehead on the 27th July 1983 Mr. Sterry after a short period of time (over which there is some dispute) resumed contact with Matthew and upon his return to Garden City in September of 1983 began to see Matthew every other day, a frequency which has been maintained to date.

Whilst working at Minehead Mr. Sterry met a young woman called Mamie Joyce Hanley probably in the August of 1983. In February 1984 Mr. Sterry and Miss Hanley began to cohabit at 18 Brookside Garden City. They claim to have a stable relationship and Miss Hanley stated in evidence that she was able and willing to care for the child as her own. Miss Hanley also stated in evidence -significantly- that she and Mr. Sterry had only seen each other twice since they first met in August 1983 and when they began to cohabit in February 1984. The Welfare Report was prepared by a Mrs. Underwood of Clwyd County Council Social Services Department. She had too many reservations about Mr. Sterry's past behaviour to conclude that his present relationship with Miss Hanley would prove to be any more stable than that with Miss Edge. In the event Mrs. Underwood felt unable to make any positive recommendation

179

to the Justices. The only suggestion was that - if the Justices did decide to award the custody of Matthew to Mr. Sterry - it should be accompanied by a supervision order. Significantly Mrs. Underwood was unaware when she prepared her report/that Mr. Sterry and Miss Hanley had met only twice before cohabiting in February 1984. In the event the Justices ordered the custody of Matthew to Mr. Sterry together with a supervision order to the Court Probation Service. The order was suspended for 28 days to allow time for the consideration of an appeal or any other appropriate form of action.

Miss Edge has maintained throughout that she wants a Care Order to be made with respect to Matthew and sees long-term fostering and/or adoption as the solution most conducive to Matthew's best interests. She vehemently denies that she is motivated in any way by malice. Her fears are that if Mr. Sterry ultimately obtains the custody of Matthew his past behaviour is likely to recur. It seems clear from the evidence given at the hearing before the Justices that Mr. Sterry is given to creating responsibilities for himself and others and then abandoning them. In 1981 he made Miss Edge pregnant and then had the pregnancy terminated. He has had another child by a Miss Tina Moody of Chester which he now rarely sees. It is also clear that having taken on family responsibilities with Miss Edge and Matthew he abandoned them with minimal financial support and made no attempt to prevent Matthew from being taken into care on either occasion. In addition Miss Edge does not view his present relationship with Miss Hanley as a sufficiently stable one for the custody of Matthew to be safely committed to them. Her fears seem to be genuine in that they are borne out by the inability of Mrs. Underwood to make any positive recommendation to the Justices either in her report or in evidence. Miss Edge is therefore unhappy about the result of the hearing before the Justices and I am therefore asked to advise on the appropriate method of appeal.

An appeal against the order of the Justices would be to the Divisional Court of the High Court (see Section 16 (3) of the Guardianship of Minors Act 1971 and R.S.C. Order 55 (a)). Such an appeal is by way of a re-hearing and is brought by way of Originating Motion. A further application to the single Judge of the High Court would have to be made in order to stay the order of the Justices pending the outcome of this appeal. I am however unhappy about persuing an appeal under the 1971 Act. The machinery of the Act is geared to a custody contest which, on the facts of this case, is a little atificial. The Local Authority did not intervene in this application before the Justices although they are clearly involved and no-one represented the interests of the child. The appropriate forum in my view would be the Wardship jurisdiction of the High Court. The use of the office of the Official Solicitor would be particularly advantageous in this respect the object being to ensure that the Ward's point of view is represented by an experienced and impartial outsider and to insulate the child so far as possible from the effects of any conflict between the parents and to ensure that decisions are taken in the best interests of the child. There would be available to the Court any relevant expert opinions previously unavailable and the Local Authority would also be joined as a Defendant and thereby forced to take an active part in the proceedings which they have not to date. The use of the Wardship jurisdiction and its aims are consonant with instructions and desires of Miss Edge throughout the history of the matter. There is, however, authority for the proposition that the Wardship jurisdiction ought not to be invoked where there is a subsisting and effective order of the Justices (as here) unless either (a) some relief was sought which was unobtainable in that court or (b) there are exceptional circumstances: (see in Re D (Minors) (1973) 2 All E.R. 993 Bagnall J). In my view this is not the sort of situation envisaged in that case of two rival contestants for custody seeking to use the Wardship jurisdiction as an appeal forum.

Here Miss Edge does not want the custody care and control of Matthew but does not feel that Mr. Sterry is suitable to have custody care and control. She wants what is best for Matthew and in my view the Wardship jurisidction is the best forum to achieve that goal.

Miss Edge was granted Legal Aid to defend Mr. Sterry's application under the 1971 Act. To my mind there is cause for concern over this child's welfare. The hearing before the Justices took something in excess of six hours and the Welfare Report enclosed no positive recommendations owing to the considerable reservations about Mr. Sterry's suitability felt by the author. My preference, after much consideration, is for wardship as against an appeal to the Divisional Court for the reasons I have stated. In my view the interests of the child dictate that Miss Edge ought properly to be granted legal aid to pursue her wardship application and I advise that the Legal Aid Certficate be amended accordingly. Once that amendment is obtained the Originating Summons and supporting Affidavits can be drafted. I would urge upon the Law Society the urgency of the situation in that the Justices granted a stay of execution only of 28 days and a furth application to the High Court will be necessary if the order of the Justices is to be stayed pending the outcome of the Wardship proceed

P.D.

P.D. Fogarty.
Oriel Chambers,
14 Water Street,
Liverpool 2.

I am living with my mum in her flat which is situated in Bromborough village. I am the talk of the town so to speak. I am called the Witch who gave up her son. Whispers of how could a mother give up her baby.

I cannot take it anymore. I am drowning in my own tears. I am in a deep dark place. I am sinking in my own shit. My choice is to leave all this behind to try and start over.

Matthew moves back into a family home with his dad Mike and his new wife. I agree not to keep in contact so that Matthew can have a happy normal life on the condition that I am informed from time to time of how he is.

I leave to go to work and live in Jersey where I lived for four years trying to re-build my life.

Over this time, I am in regular contact with Social Services to enquire after my son. I also keep in contact with Matthew's granddad. My mum and I tried repeatedly to keep some form of contact with Matthew until he was six but to no avail.

I did get to meet my son when he was 28. He had grown into a fine young man. He had been well brought up. Sadly, our relationship didn't come to much as in 2017 he explained to me that he wanted to concentrate